INTELLECTUAL AND DEVELOPMENTAL DISABILITIES NURSING: SCOPE AND STANDARDS OF PRACTICE

nurses
books
.org

The Publishing Program of ANA

AMERICAN NURSES
ASSOCIATION

SILVER SPRING, MARYLAND
2004

AAMR

FOUNDED 1876

Library of Congress Cataloging-in-Publication data

American Association on Mental Retardation. Nursing Division.

Intellectual and developmental disabilities nursing : scope and standards of practice / Nursing Division of the American Association on Mental Retardation.

p. ; cm.

Rev ed. of: Statement on the scope and standards for the nurse who specializes in developmental disabilities and/or mental retardation / Nursing Division of the American Association on Mental Retardation [and] American Nurses Association. ©1998.

Includes bibliographical references and index.

ISBN 1-55810-223-X

1. Mental retardation—Nursing—Standards—United States. 2. Developmental disabilities—Nursing—Standards—United States. 3. Psychiatric nursing—Standards—United States.

[DNLM: 1. Developmental Disabilities—nursing. 2. Mental Retardation—nursing. 3. Clinical Competence—standards. 4. Psychiatric Nursing—methods. 5. Psychiatric Nursing—standards. WY 160 A5125i 2004] I. American Nurses Association. II. American Association on Mental Retardation. Nursing Division. Statement on the scope and standards for the nurse who specializes in developmental disabilities and/ or mental retardation. III. Title.

RC570.2.A47 2004
616.85'88'0231—dc22   2004018989

Disclaimer: The American Nurses Association (ANA) is a national professional association. This ANA publication—*Intellectual and Developmental Nursing: Scope and Standards of Practice*—reflects the thinking of the nursing profession on various issues and should be reviewed in conjunction with state board of nursing policies and practices. State law, rules, and regulations govern the practice of nursing, while *Intellectual and Developmental Nursing: Scope and Standards of Practice* guides nurses in the application of their professional skills and responsibilities.

Published by

nursesbooks.org
The Publishing Program of ANA

American Nurses Association
8515 Georgia Avenue, Suite 400
Silver Spring, MD 20910

1-800-274-4ANA (4262)

http://www.nursingworld.org/

ISBN 1-55810-223-X

04SSID   2M   09/04

ACKNOWLEDGMENTS

The Nursing Division of the American Association on Mental Retardation and the American Nurses Association would like to personally thank those who contributed their valuable time and talents to this revised edition, *Intellectual and Developmental Disabilities Nursing: Scope and Standards of Practice*. In its original (1988) edition, the document was called *Statement on the Scope and Standards for the Nurse Who Specializes in Developmental Disabilities and/or Mental Retardation*.

The authors of the *in Intellectual and Developmental Disabilities Nursing: Scope and Standards of Practice* include:

Wendy M. Nehring, RN, PhD, FAAN, FAAMR
Shirley P. Roth, RN, MSN, FAAMR
Deborah Natvig, RN, PhD
Cecily L. Betz, RN, PhD, FAAN
Teresa Savage, RN, PhD
Marilyn Krajicek, RN, EdD, FAAN

Special thanks are extended to Lee Barks, RN, MS, ARNP, and Sally Colatarci, RN, MS for their suggestions.

ANA Staff

Carol Bickford, PhD, RN,BC – Content Editor
Yvonne Humes, MSA
Winifred Carson-Smith, JD

Contents

PREFACE

The American Nurses Association (ANA) has been the vanguard for nursing practice for more than a century. *Code of Ethics for Nurses with Interpretive Statements* (ANA 2001), *Nursing: Scope and Standards of Practice* (ANA 2004), and *Nursing's Social Policy Statement* (2nd ed.) (ANA 2003) are all documents that provide background for nursing standards. These documents are intended to provide the public with assurances of safe and competent nursing care. Along with these documents, specialty nursing organizations have worked with the ANA to publish specific standards of care and professional practice in their specialty.

This document, concerning the care of individuals with intellectual and developmental disabilities (hereafter referred to as I/DD), is a revision of *Statement on the Scope and Standards for the Nurse Who Specializes in Developmental Disabilities and/or Mental Retardation* (Nehring et al, 1998).

This new document has been revised to: (*i*) capture the changing practice of nursing in this specialty (i.e., encompassing all levels of education, all system levels of care from the individual to the system itself), (*ii*) emphasize the unique healthcare needs and characteristics of individuals of all ages with I/DD, and (*iii*) to incorporate the ANA standards mentioned above (ANA 2004). It should also be used in conjunction with other standards of care and professional performance developed by other specialty nursing groups [e.g., *Scope and Standards of Pediatric Nursing Practice* (Society of Pediatric Nurses & ANA 2003); *Statement on the Scope and Standards of Genetics Clinical Nursing Practice* (International Society of Nurses in Genetics, Inc. & ANA, 1998); *Scope and Standards of Public Health Nursing Practice* (ANA, 1999); *Scope and Standards of Psychiatric–Mental Health Nursing Practice* (American Psychiatric Nurses Association, International Society of Psychiatric–Mental Health Nurses, & ANA, 2000); and *Scope and Standards of Professional School Nursing Practice* (National Association of School Nurses & ANA, 2001).

In addition, adolescents and adults with I/DD and their families collaborate with healthcare professionals in making person-centered decisions about their health care. This self-advocacy has arisen in tandem with an evolving healthcare system that may or may not optimize healthcare options for all people. Therefore, in response to these changes, individuals of all ages with I/DD and their families should be assured of safe and effective nursing care. This document describes this care.

Standards of Intellectual and Developmental Disabilities (I/DD) Nursing Practice: Standards of Practice

Standard 1. Assessment
The registered nurse who specializes in I/DD collects comprehensive data pertinent to the patient's health or the situation.

Standard 2. Diagnosis
The registered nurse who specializes in I/DD analyzes the assessment data to determine the diagnoses or issues.

Standard 3. Outcomes Identification
The registered nurse who specializes in I/DD identifies expected outcomes for a plan to the patient or the situation.

Standard 4. Planning
The registered nurse who specializes in I/DD develops a plan that prescribes strategies and alternatives to attain expected outcomes.

Standard 5. Implementation
The registered nurse who specializes in I/DD implements the identified plan.

Standard 5A: Coordination of Care
The registered nurse who specializes in I/DD coordinates care delivery.

Standard 5B: Health Teaching and Health Promotion
The registered nurse who specializes in I/DD employs strategies to promote health and a safe environment.

Standard 5C: Consultation
The registered nurse and the advanced practice registered nurse who specializes in I/DD provide consultation to influence the identified plan, enhance the abilities of others, and effect change.

Standard 5D: Prescriptive Authority and Treatment
The advanced practice registered nurse who specializes in I/DD uses prescriptive authority, procedures, referrals, treatments, and therapies in accordance with state and federal laws and regulations.

Standard 6: Evaluation
The registered nurse who specializes in I/DD evaluates progress toward attainment of outcomes.

Standards of Intellectual and Developmental Disabilities (I/DD) Nursing Practice: Standards of Professional Performance

Standard 7. Quality of Practice
The registered nurse who specializes in I/DD systematically enhances the quality and effectiveness of nursing practice.

Standard 8. Education
The registered nurse who specializes in I/DD attains knowledge and competency that reflects current nursing practice.

Standard 9. Professional Practice Evaluation
The registered nurse who specializes in I/DD evaluates one's own nursing practice in relation to professional practice standards and guidelines, relevant statutes, rules, and regulations.

Standard 10. Collegiality
The registered nurse who specializes in I/DD interacts with and contributes to the professional development of peers and colleagues.

Standard 11. Collaboration
The registered nurse who specializes in I/DD collaborates with the individual with I/DD, family, and others in the conduct of nursing practice.

Standard 12. Ethics
The registered nurse who specializes in I/DD integrates ethical provisions in all areas of practice.

Standard 13. Research
The registered nurse who specializes in I/DD integrates research findings into practice.

Standard 14. Resource Utilization
The registered nurse specializing in I/DD considers factors related to safety, effectiveness, cost, and impact on practice in the planning and delivery of nursing services to individuals with I/DD.

Standard 15. Leadership
The nurse who specializes in I/DD provides leadership in the professional practice setting and the profession.

SCOPE OF PRACTICE OF INTELLECTUAL AND DEVELOPMENTAL DISABILITIES (I/DD) NURSING

Nurses who specialize in intellectual and developmental disabilities (I/DD) are unique in the population that they serve. Because this nursing specialty was primarily institutional until the late 1950s, and because of the stigma attached to this population, many nurses are not familiar with this nursing specialty. In fact, it was only recognized as such by the American Nurses Association (ANA) in 1997 (Nehring, 1999).

Unlike many nursing specialties, the scope of practice for nurses in I/DD extends across all levels of care, as well as all healthcare and many educational settings. Even though individuals with I/DD are present today in all communities and healthcare settings, they remain a vulnerable population. This is because they often need assistance to advocate for their needs and many healthcare professionals are not educated and skilled to care for their specific condition and developmental needs. Such health disparities were highlighted in the Surgeon General's report, *Closing the Gap: A National Blueprint to Improve the Health of Persons with Mental Retardation* (U.S. Public Health Service 2002). Working in an interdisciplinary context, nurses continue to strive to promote the importance of the discipline of nursing in this specialty field and to provide specific health care at both the generalist and advanced practice level.

Definition of Nursing in I/DD

Intellectual and developmental disability refers to a wide variety of mental or physical conditions that interfere with the ability of an individual to function effectively at an expected developmental level. These conditions are frequently referred to as *developmental disabilities* or *mental retardation.* A *developmental disability* is:

> a severe chronic disability of an individual that (a) is attributable to mental or physical impairment or combination of mental and physical impairments; (b) is manifested before the individual attains the age of 22; (c) is likely to continue indefinitely; (d) re-

sults in substantial functional limitations in these following areas of major life activity: self-care, receptive and expressive living, and economic self-sufficiency; and (e) reflects the individual's need for a combination and sequence of special, interdisciplinary, or generic services, individualized support, or other forms of assistance that are of lifelong or extended duration and are individually planned and coordinated (Developmental Disabilities Assistance and Bill of Rights Act of 2000).

The definition of *mental retardation* is:

a disability characterized by significant limitations both in intellectual functioning and in adaptive behavior as expressed in conceptual, social, and practical adaptive skills. This disability originates before age 18. The following five assumptions are essential to the application of this definition: (a) limitations in present functioning must be considered within the context of community environments typical of the individual's age peers and culture; (b) valid assessment considers cultural and linguistic diversity as well as differences in communication, sensory, motor, and behavioral factors; (c) within an individual, limitations often coexist with strengths; (d) an important purpose of describing limitations is to develop a profile of needed supports; and (e) with appropriate personalized supports over a sustained period, the life functioning of the person with mental retardation generally will improve. (Luckasson et al, 2002, 1).

Nurses who specialize in the care of persons of all ages with I/DD care for persons with these conditions. These conditions may be organic and nonorganic or social in nature.

It is important to clarify that I/DD is different from chronic conditions or illness and disabilities in general. *Chronic conditions* can simply mean any condition that persists over a long period. Although I/DD exists across time, the definition is more specific. This is also true for *disabilities,* a general term that refers to any condition that limits activities of daily living. Again, I/DD may limit activities of daily living, but the conditions require more specific understanding of epidemiology, etiology, diagnosis, treatment and management, follow-up, and nursing implications.

Another term often used is *children with special healthcare needs*. Children with I/DD often have special healthcare needs, but this may not be a consistent problem. For example, a child with Down syndrome may have special needs, but they may not always concern their health at any given time.

It is important, as new terminology is used, to identify and describe particular conditions (e.g., pervasive developmental disabilities and special-needs child), so that nurses do not lose sight of the knowledge and skills needed to care for persons with I/DD, regardless of the diagnosis. Although the terms to describe I/DD may overlap (i.e., developmental disabilities and special healthcare needs in the child with cerebral palsy), the definitions for developmental disabilities and mental retardation are used in federal legislation and must be understood by nurses until these definitions are altered.

Evolution of Nursing Practice in I/DD

Early education for nurses who specialized in the care of persons, of any age, with I/DD occurred both in general nursing hospital schools and in asylums and institutions. Until the early twentieth century, persons with I/DD were diagnosed as having mental illness, and their care took place in settings where persons with all forms of mental illness were housed. It was not until after World War I, when a better understanding of mental illness developed, that the care of persons with I/DD was more specifically detailed. Terminology at this time included *idiocy* and *imbecile*. In the early 1960s, President Kennedy brought needed attention to the living conditions of persons of all ages with I/DD, then called *mental retardation*. New legislation was introduced and funding became available for the first time for this population. Large institutional settings remained the primary place of residence for persons of all ages with I/DD until the late 1960s. It was the social norm to place newborns and children with known conditions resulting in I/DD in institutions as soon as possible so as not to burden the families, either financially or through social stigma.

After public attention was focused on the custodial and often inhumane care of persons with I/DD in the early 1970s, radical changes took place. Many individuals with I/DD were moved back to their homes or to newly formed community settings such as group homes, semi-independent living arrangements (SILAs), and smaller, congregate settings (e.g. 16-beds). The transition from institutional to community living varies state by state. Today, newborns with I/DD are no longer placed in institutions. Most individuals with I/DD live with their families in the community. Others live in small group community settings; only the most severely affected individuals who require substantial medical care remain in larger, developmental centers (Nehring, 1999).

Nursing care has also evolved. Early documentation about nursing care was written by physicians or nurses who cared for persons with both I/DD and mental illness. Specific literature on the nursing care of persons with I/DD written by nurses first appeared with any frequency in the 1950s. At that time, nurses in institutional settings did little more than record vital signs and occasional patient weights and give medications. Public health nurses also provided care for children with I/DD who remained at home. However, parents were often encouraged to enroll their children in institutions by the time they reached school age. The first national meeting for nurses specializing in the care of children with I/DD was sponsored by the Children's Bureau in 1958 (Nehring, 1999).

In the 1960s, nursing care in the institution resembled that of nursing care provided in hospitals. Subsequently, the role of the nurse expanded to include education and research. Clinical advanced practice registered nurses were employed by some institutions and post-baccalaureate and graduate programs emerged to provide education designed especially for the care of children and adolescents with I/DD in universities across the country. Interdisciplinary faculty (including nurses) at University-Affiliated Programs and Facilities (UAPs or UAFs) established by President Kennedy, offered education to future specialists in this field (including nurses), conducted research on topics related to mental retardation, and provided health and social services to individuals with I/DD and their families.

Also during this time, nurses began to write more prolifically about the care of children with conditions resulting in I/DD. Some of the resulting books and articles are now classics, especially for public health nurses. Developmental diagnostic clinics were established across the country to identify and refer children for developmental and health care when appropriate. Nursing consultants who specialized in this field were hired by the Children's Bureau; Division of Neurological Diseases and Stroke, U.S. Public Health Service; Mental Retardation Division, Department of Health, Education, and Welfare; Association of Retarded Children; and the United Cerebral Palsy Associations, Inc. National meetings were convened for these nursing specialists and the first standards of nursing practice for this specialty emerged in 1968, *The Guidelines for Nursing Standards in Residential Centers for the Mentally Retarded* (Haynes, 1968; Nehring, 1999).

The 1970s brought about the first legislation mandating that all children with I/DD deserved a free and appropriate public education from 3 through 21 years of age. Advanced practice roles for nurses in this specialty continued to expand, including roles in schools and early intervention programs for the infant from birth to 3 years of age. Publications and regular national and regional meetings continued to be held throughout this decade. Special courses in this specialty also began to appear in nursing programs across the country (Nehring, 1999).

The term *developmental disabilities* was first introduced during the Nixon presidency to describe conditions similar to those defined as mental retardation but that differed slightly. Interdisciplinary care was the norm in the 1980s, when all disciplines worked together with the individuals with I/DD and their family members in assessing and planning care in a variety of settings (Nehring, 1999). In 1980, the American Nurses Association published *School Nurses Working With Handicapped Children* (Igoe, Green, Heim, Licata, MacDonough, and McHugh, 1980). In the 1980s, two sets of standards of nursing practice for nurses specializing in this field emerged: *Standards of Nursing Practice in Mental Retardation/Developmental Disabilities* (Aggen and Moore, 1984) and *Standards for the Clinical Advanced Practice Registered Nurse in Developmental Disabilities/Handicapping Conditions* (Austin, Challela, Huber, Sciarillo, and Stade, 1987).

Emphasis on the adult with I/DD emerged in the nursing literature in the 1990s. An examination of the individual with I/DD across the lifespan was first highlighted in *A Life-Span Approach to Nursing Care for Individuals with Developmental Disabilities* (Roth and Morse, 1994). Nursing standards for this field were also revised: *Standards of Developmental Disabilities Nursing Practice* (Aggen et al., 1995) and *Statement on the Scope and*

Standards for the Nurse Who Specializes in Developmental Disabilities and/ or Mental Retardation (Nehring et al., 1998). Other related standards of nursing practice in early intervention (Consensus Committee, 1993), care of children and adolescents with special health and developmental needs (Consensus Committee, 1994), and genetics (International Society of Nurses in Genetics, Inc. and ANA, 1998) were written.

In the first years of the twenty-first century, a greater effort in providing educational materials for nursing students and nurses in practice who care for persons of all ages with I/DD has emerged. The Nursing Division of the American Association on Mental Retardation and the Developmental Disabilities Nurses Association have been developing separate, but complementary, projects that will provide a core curriculum for nurses and other health professionals and Internet materials, respectively.

This specialty field of nursing has changed greatly from its early years. As the healthcare system continues to evolve, so will the nursing care of persons of all ages with I/DD. Such care continues to occur in a variety of settings and at both the professional registered nurse and advanced practice registered nurse levels. Continued publications and research into such nursing care are needed as well as additional didactic and clinical content materials for nursing students.

Integrating the Science and Art of Nursing in I/DD

Like the discipline of nursing in general, the nursing specialty of I/DD is based on the nursing process whereby critical thinking is used to assess and identify health problems, determine desired outcomes, plan and act, and evaluate the nursing care. Nursing care in this specialty is defined by the standards of nursing practice and professional performance for nurses who specialize in I/DD (see Figure 1 on the following page).

The art of nursing in this specialty is also dynamic and encompasses a holistic approach in providing care. For example, the person with I/DD may have difficulty communicating or be unable to communicate. Thus, the nurse must have skills to understand and interpret the signs or signals that the individual with I/DD uses to communicate their wants and desires.

Figure 1. The Phenomena of Concern for Nurses Who Specialize in I/DD

Individuals
- Unique anatomical, physiological, and psychological differences depending on diagnosis (e.g., genetic syndromes, congenital defects, physical deformities).
- Developmental interventions based on developmental or functional rather than chronological age.
- Prevention of secondary impairments.
- Adequate and appropriate primary health care and immunizations based on chronological age.
- Appropriate management of acute and chronic illnesses.
- Consistent collaboration with the individual regarding management of health care (person-centered care).
- Appropriate healthcare teaching at the individual's developmental level.
- Holistic management of psychosocial concerns; i.e. caring for the whole person.
- Developing, implementing, and evaluating the Individualized Family Service Plan (IFSP), Individualized Education Plan (IEP), Individualized Health Plan (IHP), Individualized Plan for Employment (IPE), or Individualized Transition Plan (ITP) with the interdisciplinary team which includes the person with I/DD and their family members.
- Advocacy.
- Legal issues or concerns.
- Respect for cultural, religious, and socioeconomic differences.

Family
- Family-centered approach that is respectful of cultural, religious, and socioeconomic differences.
- Continuous collaboration with family members regarding management of health care.
- Advocacy.
- Sensitivity to family concerns that support quality of life for persons with I/DD.

Community
- Case management across the person's lifespan.
- Keeping abreast of advances in nursing and the other disciplines involved in the care of persons with I/DD.
- Economic and political changes and their influence on financial status of the family (e.g. changes in SSI policy).
- Keeping abreast of political and policy changes and being able to translate these changes to the individual and their family.

Ethical issues are very important to understanding and caring for the person with I/DD. In general, people with I/DD should no longer be seen as vulnerable and dependent. They should be viewed as self-advocates who may need some level of support to function in society. The medical model of disability views the disability as a problem within the person, to be cured or ameliorated by professionals of medicine or other social institutions, and views the disability negatively (Williams 2001, 125-7). By contrast, the social model of disability views disability as a socially constructed phenomenon in which an impairment becomes a disability when physical, social, or attitudinal barriers prevent the person from attaining goals. The disability is seen as neutral and not from a value-laden perspective. The person may require accommodation to function and attain goals (Asch 2001, 300).

The nurse respects and facilitates the person's autonomy and decision-making capacity. Even individuals with guardians should be involved in their healthcare decisions to the extent of their ability to participate in decision-making. Nurses recognize that the current healthcare system has constraints, and they must advocate and work within the limits to allow the individual with I/DD to have choices. However, the trend toward limited guardianship rather than plenary guardianship indicates that the person with I/DD is approaching equality in society.

With increasing medical and assistive technology, gains have been made in health and functional status for people with I/DD. Technology has also posed threats, as bioethicists have challenged the use of technology for persons with "severe" I/DD (Nerney 2000, 15–20). Futility policies for persons with significant cognitive impairment have been instituted (Burling 2002), and medical decision-making guidelines for withholding resuscitation of infants who are extremely premature or born with congenital anomalies have been proposed (Colorado Collective for Medical Decisions, 1999). These activities display a bias against people with I/DD, even those who are at risk for I/DD. Nurses should advocate for a careful evaluation of the benefits and burdens of a proposed treatment for a person with I/DD (or at risk for I/DD) and not accept a categorical denial of treatment based on another's estimation of the quality of life of the person with or at risk for I/DD.

The Human Genome Project also poses gains and threats to people with I/DD. Sometime in the future, the basis for I/DD may be identified and eventually "treated" with gene therapy. If this technology evolves, there may be social pressure to submit to the treatment to ameliorate or eliminate the disability, showing less tolerance for the spectrum of human difference. Already there is an assumption if a prenatal disability is detected, the mother (or parents) will elect to terminate the pregnancy. Nurses respect the autonomous decisions of the mother, but also grant that the mother's decision may be influenced by the treatment of people with I/DD within society and its lack of tolerance for difference.

As stated in *Nursing's Social Policy Statement* (2003), "Human experience is contextually and culturally defined" (2). Nurses should be mindful of the experience of people with I/DD in society as one of oppression and denial of equality. Health services such as routine gynecological care, mammograms, and preventative and therapeutic dental services should be accessible to people with I/DD. There should be a balance between *undertreatment*—the limitations of treatment based on the I/DD diagnosis—and *overtreatment*—the unwillingness to recognize when treatment is no longer beneficial. Nurses may have advocacy and educator roles in the decision-making process with the person, if capable, the family, if appropriate, and others involved in the person's care.

In addition to the significant ethical concerns and issues, nurses must be knowledgeable of psychological, social, economic, cultural, and legal issues. Nurses must grasp the interdisciplinary nature of health care in this field and be prepared to provide case management of individuals with I/DD. Nurses at any level of practice must also be active in nursing and specialty organizations at local, regional, national, or international levels. Nursing leadership is important in these organizations at all levels, as well as in the communities.

Professional Registered Nurses Who Specialize in I/DD

In the United States, professional registered nurses receive their education through three routes: associate degree (2 years), diploma (3 years), or baccalaureate degree (4 years). This education prepares the professional registered nurse to practice in a variety of specialties and settings. In these educational programs, the nursing student receives didactic and clinical experiences in I/DD, but does not specialize in this area as part of their pre-licensure program.

All nurses will care for an individual with I/DD at some time in their careers. Each person with I/DD is a person first, just like everyone else, and their healthcare needs are unique to that individual. It is important that nurses recognize that a person with I/DD:

- is not ill based on their diagnosis of a I/DD,

- does not necessarily have all of the secondary conditions identified as common to their diagnosis (e.g. a person with spina bifida does not always have hydrocephaly), and

- experiences many of the same life events (e.g. graduation, first job, etc.) and has the same feelings that all of us do.

It is important to avoid diagnostic overshadowing (attributing a health problem to the person's diagnosis of I/DD; e.g. an adolescent with Down syndrome who is depressed because they broke up with their girlfriend is thought to be depressed because they have Down syndrome). In most pre-license nursing programs, the attention to the care of persons with I/DD is small, but nurses practicing as registered nurses must be able to provide holistic care to this population. Many books, articles, videos, and Internet sites are available to assist in this learning. The registered nurse may also want to consult with a nurse specialist in this field.

The professional registered nurse who specializes in I/DD provides care to individuals, families, and groups in a wide range of care settings with an understanding of the concepts and strategies of nursing practice in this area. The professional registered nurse participates in individual and family assessment and in the planning, implementation, and evaluation of their health and health services. The professional registered nurse may serve as a case manager as part of an interdisciplinary team with individuals with I/DD who have less complex needs if an advanced practice registered nurse is not available. The professional registered nurse collaborates and consults with the advanced practice registered nurse in I/DD as a resource. If no advanced practice registered nurse is available in the practice setting, advanced practice registered nurses who can serve as consultants may be available through the Nursing Division of the American Association on Mental Retardation or through University Centers of Excellence in Developmental Disabilities (UCEDDs, formerly UAPs or UAFs).

Certification as a certified developmental disabilities nurse is available from the Developmental Disabilities Nurses Association. One requirement for taking the certification examination is 4000 hours experience working as a professional registered nurse in a setting with individuals with I/DD in the past 5 years.

Advanced Practice Registered Nurses Who Specialize in I/DD

The majority of advanced practice professional nurses will care for persons with I/DD in their careers. The nurse practitioner may encounter the pregnant woman with I/DD, the birth of a child with I/DD, the diagnosis of I/DD in a child, the care of the child with I/DD throughout childhood and adolescence to the transition to adulthood and adult health care, adult health services, psychiatric–mental health services, and finally, older adult services. The nurse practitioner may carry out these services in the clinic, hospital, school, home, or residential setting. The clinical nurse specialist, in any area of specialty, may encounter a person with I/DD in the hospital or clinic setting. The nurse midwife will most likely be involved someday in the birth of a child with I/DD or care for a woman with I/DD who is having a baby. The nurse anesthetist may also care for an individual with I/DD who is undergoing surgery.

As in pre-licensure nursing education, little attention is given to the healthcare needs of persons with I/DD in graduate nursing programs, unless the student chooses to specialize in this field. All nurses, regardless of educational preparation, must be prepared for the unique healthcare needs of persons with I/DD and always include the individual's family and additional support persons, if applicable, in all discussions of care. As stated, there are many resources available to nurses to enhance their knowledge and skills in this area, including consultation with master's and doctorally prepared nurse specialists.

It is recommended that the nurse who would like to specialize in I/DD in either their master's or doctoral program needs to attend a nursing program that is located at the same university where a UCEDD is located. Fellowships are usually available at UCEDDs for interdisciplinary education. The nursing master's student would be able to take interdisciplinary didactic courses at the UCEDD and participate in clinical practicums that involve individuals with I/DD and their families. The nursing doctoral student could also participate in the didactic interdisciplinary courses as cognates and plan and conduct their dissertation research with the assistance of the UCEDD faculty. If this is not possible, it is important for the nurse wishing to specialize in I/DD to inquire of the nursing faculty at the university that they would like to attend about how they could obtain needed interdisciplinary courses and clinical experiences. It would be very important that at least one nursing faculty be an expert in I/DD.

The master's or doctorally prepared nurse who specializes in I/DD is an advanced practice registered nurse or specialist who is capable of, and has the authority to perform, all of the functions of the professional registered nurse with a more independent and sophisticated conceptually grounded focus.

- The master's prepared nurse in this specialty may be clinically employed in the role of clinical advanced practice registered nurse, nurse consultant, nurse practitioner, nurse educator, or nurse administrator.

- The doctorally prepared nurse in this specialty may function in a clinical, educational, administrative, consultative, or research role. In addition, the advanced practice registered nurse possesses substantial experience with individuals with I/DD, their families, and community resources; skill in the formulation and implementation of social policy and legislation affecting persons with I/DD; the ability to plan, implement, and evaluate programs designed to serve individuals with I/DD and their families; and their ability to conduct research.

These skills are based on knowledge of specific I/DD, including their epidemiology and demographics. The advanced practice registered nurse understands the use of technology for persons with I/DD as well as the impact of social, psychological, educational, cultural, and religious values on individuals, their families, and communities. The advanced practice registered nurse in I/DD must be knowledgeable about cost containment, legislation, and policy planning to provide preventive, supportive, and restorative care to individuals with I/DD across the lifespan in a wide variety of settings.

The advanced practice registered nurse is prepared to engage in interdisciplinary assessments, interventions, and teaching with an emphasis on individual- and family-centered services delivered within a community context. The advanced practice registered nurse is also able to serve as a case manager and interdisciplinary team leader, and to identify and develop a program of research relevant to the practice of nursing in I/DD. This document emphasizes the development and maintenance of skills necessary to promote positive health outcomes for the entire population of individuals with I/DD; it does not focus on a particular clinical diagnosis.

Settings for Nursing Practice in I/DD

Nursing in I/DD is the care of persons with I/DD and their families across a variety of healthcare, educational, and residential settings. These settings include large public and private agencies (such as hospitals, clinics, public health clinics, worksites, and schools), small community-based facilities, large regional developmental centers, foster homes, and biological homes. The nurse who practices in this specialty may serve in several capacities, including (a) clinician, (b) teacher, (c) interdisciplinary team member, (d) case manager, (e) advocate, (f) counselor, (g) consultant, (h) administrator, and (i) researcher (Nehring, 2003). Nurses who specialize in I/DD have a broad range of concerns in providing holistic care to individuals, families, and communities (see Figure 1).

Continued Commitment to the Nursing Specialty of I/DD

The nurse's practice in I/DD is both independent and collaborative. Under professional licensure, the nurse's independent responsibility is screening, the formulation of nursing diagnosis, the care of human responses to health and illness, and the evaluation of individual and family outcomes (ANA 2004). The guiding principles for nurses to provide a continuum of services to individuals with I/DD across the lifespan include:

- Collaborative, comprehensive, and coordinated care;
- Cultural competence;
- Developmental appropriateness;
- Family-/youth-/person-centered care;
- Inclusiveness; and
- Normalization.

Each of these terms is defined in the glossary. Nurses in I/DD further provide services that incorporate system assessment, policy development and implementation, and quality assurance.

Nurses remain in this specialty because their passion is the care of individuals with I/DD. There are many challenges and rewards in this field. Advances in science, especially in genetics and diagnostic technology, provide new insights and understanding of different conditions, their etiology, their trajectory, possible secondary conditions, and strategies for the management of the individual's health care so that quality of life can be and remain optimal. Learning about and caring for individuals with I/DD often enlighten and add meaning to one's nursing care.

Nurses who specialize in this field learn that we all are more alike than we are different. Nurses learn to appreciate an individual's strengths and assist the individual to cope and function with their limitations. Challenges include a multitude of healthcare problems that require many treatments or medications, uncertainty of the future because healthcare professionals do not know all there is to know about these conditions across the lifespan and especially in middle and late adulthood, and frustration with a society that thinks of persons with I/DD as different. There is a place for this nursing specialty and there always will be persons with I/DD who need to have someone care about and for their healthcare needs.

Professional Trends and Issues in I/DD

Currently, nurses in I/DD are involved through their practice and advocacy in a number of issues: predominant cultural concerns, early assessment and identification, inclusion in the school setting, adult health care, transition, self-advocacy and self-determination, employment, community living, managed care, and genetics. As nurses care for persons with I/DD and their families from diverse backgrounds, culturally competent methods of communication, care, and intervention must be developed and evaluated.

Nurses play a key role in the healthcare management of the person with I/DD throughout their life. Especially important is the transition from pediatric to adult healthcare services—ensuring that persons with I/DD living in a variety of residential settings, including the biological home, receive regular, quality health care, and that adolescents and adults with I/DD learn to advocate for themselves. New discoveries in the human genome have created vast opportunities for nurses to improve case identification, coordination, and referral; education;

identification, prevention, and management of primary and secondary disease conditions; and evaluation and follow-up of such conditions.

There is also a nursing shortage in this specialty. Efforts are being made in public and private agencies to increase salaries. Nursing organizations are developing continuing education and distance learning projects, as well as a core curriculum to assist nurses in learning more about I/DD and the needed nursing care. Nurses, across time, have contributed to the field by writing books, articles, and pamphlets, directing films, and producing Internet and distance learning products, to illustrate best practices and evidence-based care for nurses.

Standards of Intellectual and Developmental Disabilities (I/DD) Nursing Practice

These standards provide direction for nurses specializing in this field, provide a foundation for evaluation of nursing practice, and represent the current level of knowledge and practice in that specialty. These standards apply to both the professional registered nurse and advanced practice registered nurse in I/DD. In the absence of the advanced practice registered nurse, the professional registered nurse assumes much, but not all, of the more comprehensive role of the advanced practice registered nurse. The authors recommend that the professional registered nurse level include nurses who are educationally prepared at the baccalaureate level. These standards apply to the nursing care of persons with I/DD of all ages, cultures, socioeconomic backgrounds, and medical diagnoses. Furthermore, these standards apply to any healthcare, education, residential, or community setting where individuals with I/DD might be.

Standards of practice for any specialty must be dynamic and reflect the current state of knowledge and practice. Standards of practice should be assessed along with other measures (e.g. educational degrees), documents [e.g. *Nursing's Social Policy Statement* (ANA 2003) and *Nursing: Scope and Standards of Practice* (ANA 2004)], scientific evidence, and state nursing practice acts that provide guidelines for evaluating nursing practice. Standards of practice can be used:

- In practice for developing job position statements, performance evaluations, determining reimbursement ratings, and utilization review;
- In the development and validation of nursing theory and theory from related disciplines in relation to I/DD;
- In the development and testing of research questions;
- In the development, implementation, and evaluation of instruction to individuals and families by nurses or educational programs for groups of nurses, healthcare professionals, individuals with I/DD, their families, or the public;

- In the development of policy related to service, practice, and federal financing programs; and

- As clinical evidence for practice.

Each standard of practice and professional performance listed in this document has been standardized by the ANA (2004). The measurement criteria have been developed by the authors to represent quality practice and performance in the nursing care of individuals with I/DD.

Standards of Practice of Intellectual and Developmental Disabilities (I/DD) Nursing

Standard 1. Assessment
The registered nurse who specializes in I/DD collects comprehensive data pertinent to the patient's health or the situation.

Measurement Criteria

The registered nurse:

- Systematically collects data over time.

- Involves the individual with I/DD, family, other healthcare and interdisciplinary professionals and paraprofessionals, and the work and home environment, as appropriate, in obtaining comprehensive data. This may involve observation, interviewing, and the use of screening and assessment tools. Diagnostic tests may be used as part of the assessment process if the nurse has specific training in that area (e.g. developmental diagnostic testing).

- Prioritizes the data to be collected according to the immediate condition or anticipated needs, or the situation.

- Uses appropriate evidence-based assessment techniques and instruments in collecting pertinent data. This may include genetic studies, special serum screening (e.g. cystic fibrosis, Tay–Sachs, sickle-cell disease), nutritional needs and metabolic functioning, and any other condition-specific data.

- Uses analytical models and problem-solving tools that are appropriate for persons with I/DD.

- Synthesizes all data, information, and knowledge from the individual with I/DD, family members, the interdisciplinary team, and the individual's environment that is relevant to identify patterns and variances. This may involve data and information from the school, work site, or residential setting.

- Documents relevant data in a retrievable format.

Additional Measurement Criteria for the Advanced Practice Registered Nurse

The advanced practice registered nurse:

- Initiates and interprets diagnostic tests and procedures, relevant to the individual with I/DD's current status.

STANDARD 2. DIAGNOSIS
The registered nurse who specializes in I/DD analyzes the assessment data to determine the diagnoses or issues.

Measurement Criteria

The registered nurse:

- Identifies diagnoses or issues based on assessment data.

- Validates diagnoses or issues in partnership with the individual with I/DD, family, and members of the interdisciplinary team when possible and appropriate.

- Documents diagnoses or issues in a manner that facilitates the determination of the expected outcomes and plan.

Additional Measurement Criteria for the Advanced Practice Registered Nurse

The advanced practice registered nurse:

- Systematically compares and contrasts the history and clinical findings with normal and abnormal variations and developmental events in formulating differential diagnoses.

- Is aware that there may be specific values, ranges, and outcomes for a specific diagnosis (e.g. Down syndrome).

- Synthesizes all data and information collected during interview, examination, and diagnostic procedures (including developmental and supports assessment) to identify diagnoses.

- Serves as a consultant to the registered nurse and other staff in developing and maintaining competency in the diagnostic process.

Additional Measurement Criteria for the Nursing Role Specialty

The advanced practice registered nurse:

- Analyzes accessibility and availability of services, barriers to adequate health care, specific populations at high risk, health promotion needs for specific populations, and environmental hazards that may affect health.

STANDARD 3. OUTCOME IDENTIFICATION
The registered nurse who specializes in I/DD identifies expected outcomes for a plan to the patient or the situation.

Measurement Criteria
The registered nurse:

- Partners with the individual with I/DD, family, and members of the interdisciplinary team in formulating expected outcomes when possible and appropriate.

- Derives culturally appropriate expected outcomes from the diagnosis.

- Considers associated risks, benefits, and costs, current scientific evidence, and clinical expertise when formulating expected outcomes.

- Defines expected outcomes in terms of the individual with I/DD, his or her values, the values of the family members when appropriate, ethical and legal considerations, environment, or situation with such consideration as associated risks, benefits, and costs, and current scientific, ethical, and legal evidence.

- Includes a time estimate for attainment of expected outcomes.

- Develops expected outcomes that provide direction for continuity of care and person-centered care as appropriate.

- Modifies expected outcomes based on changes in status (i.e. health, social, living, economic, or legal) of the individual with I/DD or evidence of the situation.

- Documents expected outcomes as measurable goals.

Additional Measurement Criteria for the Advanced Practice Registered Nurse
The advanced practice registered nurse:

- Identifies expected outcomes that incorporate scientific evidence and are achievable through implementation of evidence-based practices.

I/DD Nursing: Scope & Standards of Practice

- Identifies expected outcomes that incorporate cost and clinical effectiveness, legal and ethical boundaries, satisfaction and understanding, and consistency and continuity among the individual with I/DD, family members, healthcare providers, and members of the interdisciplinary team.
- Supports the use of clinical guidelines linked to positive patient outcomes.

Standard 4. Planning

The registered nurse who specializes in I/DD develops a plan that prescribes strategies and alternatives to attain expected outcomes.

Measurement Criteria

The registered nurse:

- Develops an individualized plan that is person-centered when appropriate, considering individual or situational characteristics (e.g., chronological and developmental age, culturally appropriate, and least restrictive environment).

- Develops the plan in collaboration with the individual with I/DD, family, others, and the interdisciplinary team, as appropriate.

- Includes strategies within the plan that address individual identified diagnoses or issues, which may include strategies for promotion and restoration of health and prevention of illness, injury, and disease.

- Provides for continuity within the plan.

- Incorporates an implementation pathway or timeline within the plan.

- Establishes the plan priorities with the individual with I/DD, family, others, and the interdisciplinary team as appropriate.

- Utilizes the plan to provide direction to other members of the healthcare and interdisciplinary team.

- Defines the plan to reflect current federal laws, statutes, rules and regulations, and standards.

- Integrates current trends and research affecting comprehensive care for the individual with I/DD in the planning process.

- Considers the economic impact of the plan.

- Uses standardized and person-first language or other recognized terminology to document the plan.

Additional Measurement Criteria for the Advanced Practice Nurse

The advanced practice registered nurse:

- Identifies assessment, screening and diagnostic strategies, and therapeutic interventions within the plan that reflect current evidence, including data, research, literature, and expert clinical knowledge.

- Selects or designs strategies to meet the multifaceted needs of complex individuals with I/DD.

- Includes the synthesis of the individual with I/DD's values and beliefs regarding nursing, medical, social, and educational therapies within the plan.

Additional Measurement Criteria for the Nursing Role Specialty

The registered nurse in a nursing role specialty:

- Participates in the design and development of interdisciplinary processes to address the situation or the issue.

- Contributes to the development and continuous improvement of organizational systems that support the planning process.

- Supports the integration of clinical, human, and financial resources to enhance and complete the decision-making and evaluation processes.

The advanced practice registered nurse in a nursing role specialty:

- Serves as a consultant to the registered nurse in plan development, priority setting, cost–benefit analysis, and identification of resources, as needed.

- In collaboration with the registered nurse, other members of the interdisciplinary team, and in partnership with the community, derives community-focused plans that are based on identified problems, conditions, or needs and that build on the strengths of the community.

- Develops plans that ensure continuity of care and minimize or eliminate gaps in and duplication of services.

Standard 5. Implementation
The registered nurse who specializes in I/DD implements the identified plan.

Measurement Criteria
The registered nurse:

- Implements the plan in a safe and timely manner.

- Documents implementation and any modifications, including changes or omissions, of the identified plan.

- Utilizes evidence-based interventions and treatments specific to the diagnosis or problem.

- Utilizes community resources and systems to implement the plan.

- Collaborates with nursing colleagues and others to implement the plan.

Additional Measurement Criteria for the Advanced Practice Registered Nurse
The advanced practice registered nurse:

- Facilitates utilization of systems and community resources to implement the plan.

- Supports collaboration with nursing colleagues and other members of the interdisciplinary team to implement the plan.

- Incorporates new knowledge and strategies to initiate change in nursing care practices if desired outcomes are not achieved.

Additional Measurement Criteria for the Nursing Role Specialty
The registered nurse in a nursing role specialty:

- Implements the plan using principles and concepts of project or systems management.

- Fosters organizational systems that support implementation of the plan.

STANDARD 5A: COORDINATION OF CARE
The registered nurse who specializes in I/DD coordinates delivery of care.

Measurement Criteria
The registered nurse:

- Coordinates implementation of the plan.
- Documents the coordination of the care.

Measurement Criteria for the Advanced Practice Registered Nurse
The advanced practice registered nurse:

- Provides leadership in the coordination of interdisciplinary health care for integrated delivery of patient care services.
- Synthesizes data and information to prescribe necessary system and community support measures, including environmental modifications.
- Coordinates system and community resources that enhance delivery of care across continuums.

Additional Measurement Criteria for the Nursing Role Specialty
The registered nurse in a nursing role specialty:

- Makes referrals to other disciplines as needed.
- Supervises or provides direction to ancillary and unlicensed personnel who provide health care to individuals with I/DD and their families.
- Keeps the individual and family (and direct care support professionals when present) informed about their health status.
- Keeps the individual and the family informed about healthcare resources that are available.
- Employs strategies to promote health in a safe and least restrictive environment in home and community settings.

STANDARD 5B: HEALTH TEACHING AND HEALTH PROMOTION
The registered nurse who specializes in I/DD employs strategies to promote health and a safe environment.

Measurement Criteria

The registered nurse:

- Provides health teaching that addresses such topics as healthy lifestyles, risk-reducing behaviors, developmental needs, activities of daily living, self-care concepts and skills, and preventive self-care.

- Uses health promotion and health teaching methods appropriate to the situation and the individual with I/DD's developmental level, learning needs, readiness, ability to learn, language preference, and culture.

- Seeks opportunities for feedback and evaluation of the effectiveness of the strategies used.

Additional Measurement Criteria for the Advanced Practice Registered Nurse

The advanced practice registered nurse:

- Synthesizes empirical evidence on risk behaviors, learning theories, behavioral change theories, motivational theories, epidemiology, and other related theories and frameworks when designing health information and patient education.

- Designs health information and patient education appropriate to the individual with I/DD's developmental level, learning needs, readiness to learn, and cultural values and beliefs.

- Evaluates health information resources, such as the Internet, within the area of practice for accuracy, readability, and comprehensibility to help individuals with I/DD, family, and other members of the interdisciplinary team access quality health information.

STANDARD 5C: CONSULTATION

The registered nurse and the advanced practice registered nurse who specializes in I/DD provide consultation to influence the identified plan, enhance the abilities of others, and effect change.

Measurement Criteria for the Advanced Practice Registered Nurse

The advanced practice registered nurse:

- Synthesizes clinical data, theoretical frameworks, and evidence when providing consultation.

- Facilitates the effectiveness of a consultation by involving the individual with I/DD and family in decision-making and negotiating role responsibilities.

- Communicates consultation recommendations that facilitate change.

Additional Measurement Criteria for the Nursing Role Specialty

The registered nurse in a nursing role specialty:

- Synthesizes data, information, theoretical frameworks, and evidence when providing consultation.

- Facilitates the effectiveness of a consultation by involving the stakeholders in the decision-making process.

- Communicates consultation recommendations that influence the identified plan, facilitate understanding by involving stakeholders, enhance the work of others, and effect change.

The advanced practice registered nurse in a nursing role specialty:

- Formulates and influences health and social policies that affect individuals with I/DD.

Standard 5D: Prescriptive Authority and Treatment
The advanced practice registered nurse who specializes in I/DD uses prescriptive authority, procedures, referrals, treatments, and therapies in accordance with state and federal laws and regulations.

Measurement Criteria for the Advanced Practice Registered Nurse

The advanced practice registered nurse:

- Prescribes evidenced-based treatments, therapies, and procedures, considering the individual with I/DD's comprehensive healthcare needs.

- Prescribes pharmacological agents based on a current knowledge of pharmacology and physiology.

- Prescribes specific pharmacological agents and/or treatments based on clinical indicators, the individual with I/DD's status and needs, and the results of diagnostic and laboratory tests.

- Evaluates therapeutic and potential adverse effects of pharmacological and nonpharmacological treatments.

- Provides individuals with I/DD and their families with information about intended effects and potential adverse effects of proposed prescriptive therapies.

- Provides information about costs as well as alternative treatments and procedures, as appropriate.

Additional Measurement Criteria for the Nursing Role Specialty

The advanced practice registered nurse in a nursing role specialty:

- Provides information and makes recommendations about changes needed in health policies, regulations, and laws affecting care provided by advanced practice registered nurses for individuals with I/DD.

STANDARD 6: EVALUATION
The registered nurse who specializes in I/DD evaluates progress toward attainment of outcomes.

Measurement Criteria

The registered nurse:

- Conducts a systematic, ongoing, and criterion-based evaluation of the outcomes in relation to the structures and processes prescribed by the plan and the indicated timeline.

- Includes the individual with I/DD and others involved in the care or situation in the evaluative process.

- Evaluates the effectiveness of the planned strategies in relation to individual with I/DD's responses and the attainment of the expected outcomes.

- Documents the results of the evaluation.

- Using ongoing assessment data to revise the diagnoses, outcomes, the plan, and the implementation as needed.

- Disseminates the results to the individual with I/DD and others involved in the care or situation, as appropriate, in accordance with state and federal laws and regulations.

Additional Measurement Criteria for the Advanced Practice Registered Nurse

The advanced practice registered nurse:

- Evaluates the accuracy of the diagnoses and effectiveness of the interventions in relationship to the individual with I/DD's attainment of expected outcomes.

- Synthesizes the results of the evaluation analyses to determine the impact of the plan on the affected individuals with I/DD, families, groups, communities, and institutions.

- Uses the results of the evaluation analyses to make or recommend process or structural changes, including policy, procedure, or protocol documentation, as appropriate.

Additional Measurement Criteria for the Nursing Role Specialty

The registered nurse in a nursing role specialty:

- Uses the results of the evaluation analyses to make or recommend process or structural changes, including policy, procedure, or protocol documentation, as appropriate.

- Synthesizes the results of the evaluation analyses to determine the impact of the plan on the affected individuals with I/DD, families, groups, communities, institutions, networks, and organizations.

Standards of Professional Performance of Intellectual and Developmental Disabilities (I/DD) Nursing

Standard 7. Quality of Practice
The registered nurse who specializes in I/DD systematically enhances the quality and effectiveness of nursing practice.

Measurement Criteria
The registered nurse:

- Demonstrates quality by documenting the application of the nursing process in a responsible, accountable, and ethical manner.

- Uses the results of quality improvement activities to initiate changes in nursing practice and in the healthcare delivery system.

- Uses creativity and innovation in nursing practice to improve care delivery.

- Incorporates new knowledge to initiate changes in nursing practice if desired outcomes are not achieved.

- Participates in quality improvement activities. Such activities may include:

  - Identifying aspects of practice important for quality monitoring.

  - Using indicators developed to monitor quality and effectiveness of nursing practice.

  - Collecting data to monitor quality and effectiveness of nursing practice.

  - Analyzing quality data to identify opportunities for improving nursing practice.

  - Formulating recommendations to improve nursing practice or outcomes.

- Implementing activities to enhance the quality of nursing practice.

- Developing, implementing, and evaluating policies, procedures, and guidelines to improve the quality of practice.

- Participating on interdisciplinary teams to evaluate clinical care or health services.

- Participating in efforts to minimize costs and unnecessary duplication.

- Analyzing factors related to safety, satisfaction, effectiveness, and cost-benefit options.

- Analyzing organizational systems for barriers.

- Implementing processes to remove or decrease barriers within organizational systems.

Additional Measurement Criteria for the Advanced Practice Registered Nurse

The advanced practice registered nurse:

- Obtains and maintains professional certification if available in the area of expertise.

- Designs quality improvement initiatives.

- Implements initiatives to evaluate the need for change.

- Evaluates the practice environment and quality of nursing care rendered in relation to existing evidence, identifying opportunities for the generation and use of research.

Additional Measurement Criteria for the Nursing Role Specialty

The registered nurse in a nursing role specialty:

- Obtains and maintains professional certification if available in the area of expertise.

- Designs quality improvement initiatives.

- Implements initiatives to evaluate the need for change.

- Evaluates the practice environment in relation to existing evidence identifying opportunities for the generation and use of research in the care of individuals with I/DD.

- Evaluates nursing care delegated to other professionals, direct care support professionals, unlicensed assistive personnel, or the family and documents the effect of delegation on health outcomes.

- Participates in professional organizations which strive to improve the quality of nursing care and other services provided to individuals with I/DD and their families.

STANDARD 8. EDUCATION
The registered nurse who specializes in I/DD attains knowledge and competency that reflect current nursing practice.

Measurement Criteria

The registered nurse:

- Participates in ongoing educational activities related to appropriate knowledge bases and professional issues.

- Demonstrates a commitment to lifelong learning through self-reflection and inquiry to identify learning needs.

- Seeks experiences that reflect current practice to maintain skills and competence in clinical practice or role performance.

- Acquires knowledge and skills appropriate to the specialty area, practice setting, role, or situation.

- Maintains professional records that provide evidence of competency and lifelong learning.

- Seeks experiences and formal and independent learning activities to maintain and develop clinical and professional skills and knowledge.

Additional Measurement Criteria for the Advanced Practice Registered Nurse

The advanced practice registered nurse:

- Uses current healthcare research findings and other evidence to expand clinical knowledge, enhance role performance, and increase knowledge of professional issues.

Additional Measurement Criteria for the Nursing Role Specialty

The registered nurse in a nursing role specialty:

- Uses current research findings and other evidence related to the care of individuals with I/DD, to expand knowledge, enhance role performance, and increase knowledge of professional issues.

STANDARD 9. PROFESSIONAL PRACTICE EVALUATION

The registered nurse who specializes in I/DD evaluates one's own nursing practice in relation to professional practice standards and guidelines, relevant statutes, rules, and regulations.

Measurement Criteria

The registered nurse's practice reflects the application of knowledge of current practice standards, guidelines, statutes, rules, and regulations.

The registered nurse:

- Provides chronologically and developmentally age-appropriate care in a culturally and ethnically sensitive manner.

- Engages in self-evaluation of practice on a regular basis, identifying areas of strength, as well as areas in which professional development would be beneficial.

- Obtains informal feedback regarding one's own practice from individuals with I/DD, family members, peers, professional colleagues, and others, including direct care support professionals.

- Participates in systematic peer review as appropriate.

- Takes action to achieve goals identified during the evaluation process.

- Provides rationales for practice beliefs, decisions, and actions as part of the informal and formal evaluation processes.

Additional Measurement Criteria for the Advanced Practice Registered Nurse

The advanced practice registered nurse

- Engages in a formal process, seeking feedback regarding one's own practice from individuals with I/DD, family members, peers, professional colleagues, and others, including direct care support professionals.

Additional Measurement Criteria for the Nursing Role Specialty

The registered nurse in a nursing role specialty

- Engages in a formal process, seeking feedback regarding one's own practice from individuals with I/DD, family members, peers, professional colleagues, and others, including direct care support professionals.

STANDARD 10. COLLEGIALITY
The registered nurse who specializes in I/DD interacts with, and contributes to the professional development of, peers and colleagues.

Measurement Criteria
The registered nurse:

- Shares knowledge and skills with peers and colleagues as evidenced by such activities as patient care conferences or presentations at formal or informal meetings.

- Provides peers with feedback regarding their practice or role performance.

- Interacts with peers and colleagues to enhance one's own professional nursing practice or role performance.

- Maintains compassionate and caring relationships with peers and colleagues.

- Contributes to an environment that is conducive to the education of healthcare and other professionals that compose the interdisciplinary team.

- Contributes to a supportive and healthy work environment.

Additional Measurement Criteria for the Advanced Practice Registered Nurse
The advanced practice registered nurse:

- Models expert practice to interdisciplinary team members and healthcare consumers.

- Mentors other registered nurses and colleagues as appropriate.

- Participates with interdisciplinary teams that contribute to role development and advanced nursing practice and health care.

Additional Measurement Criteria for the Nursing Role Specialty

The registered nurse in a nursing role specialty:

- Participates on interdisciplinary teams that contribute to role development and, directly or indirectly, advance nursing practice and health services.

- Mentors other registered nurses, direct care support professionals, and colleagues as appropriate.

Standard 11. Collaboration
The registered nurse who specializes in I/DD collaborates with the individual with I/DD, family, and others in the conduct of nursing practice.

Measurement Criteria
The registered nurse:

- Communicates with the individual with I/DD, family, members of the interdisciplinary team, and healthcare providers regarding patient care and the nurse's role in the provision of that care.

- Collaborates in creating a documented plan, focused on outcomes and decisions related to care and delivery of services, that indicates communication with individuals with I/DD, families, and others.

- Partners with others to effect change and generate positive outcomes through knowledge of the individual with I/DD or situation.

- Documents referrals, including provisions for continuity of care.

Additional Measurement Criteria for the Advanced Practice Registered Nurse
The advanced practice registered nurse:

- Partners with other disciplines to enhance the care of individuals with I/DD through interdisciplinary activities, such as education, consultation, management, technological development, or research opportunities.

- Facilitates an interdisciplinary process with other members of the interdisciplinary and healthcare team.

- Documents plan of care communications, rationales for plan of care changes, and collaborative discussions to improve the care of individuals with I/DD.

Additional Measurement Criteria for the Nursing Role Specialty

The registered nurse in a nursing role specialty:

- Partners with others to enhance health care and, ultimately, care of the individual with I/DD, through interdisciplinary activities such as education, consultation, management, technological development, or research opportunities.

- Documents plans, communications, rationales for plan changes, and collaborative discussions.

- Collaborates with the individual with I/DD and family or significant others, and supports the efforts of patients and families to make appropriate decisions about utilization of resources.

The advanced practice registered nurse in a nursing role specialty:

- Participates with other interdisciplinary administrative team members in policy-making and in overall agency and community planning, implementation, and evaluation of services to and programs for individuals with I/DD.

Standard 12. Ethics
The registered nurse who specializes in I/DD integrates ethical provisions in all areas of practice.

Measurement Criteria
The registered nurse:

- Uses *Code of Ethics for Nurses with Interpretive Statements* (ANA 2001) to guide practice.

- Delivers care in a manner that preserves and protects the autonomy, dignity, and rights of individuals with I/DD.

- Maintains confidentiality of the individual with I/DD within legal and regulatory parameters.

- Serves as an advocate for the individual with I/DD by assisting them in developing skills for self-advocacy.

- Maintains a therapeutic and professional patient–nurse relationship with appropriate professional role boundaries.

- Demonstrates a commitment to practicing self-care, managing stress, and connecting with self and others.

- Contributes to resolving ethical issues of individuals with I/DD, colleagues, or systems as evidenced in such activities as participating on ethics committees.

- Reports illegal, incompetent, or impaired practices.

Additional Measurement Criteria for the Advanced Practice Registered Nurse
The advanced practice registered nurse:

- Informs the individual with I/DD and family members of the risks, benefits, and outcomes of healthcare regimens.

- Participates in interdisciplinary teams that address ethical risks, benefits, and outcomes.

Additional Measurement Criteria for the Nursing Role Specialty

The registered nurse in a nursing role specialty:

- Participates on interdisciplinary teams that address ethical risks, benefits, and outcomes.

- Informs administrators or others of the risks, benefits, and outcomes of programs and decisions that affect healthcare delivery.

- Respects the individual with I/DD's right to self-determination and includes the individual in decisions unless the individual's incapacity to participate in a specific decision is demonstrated. Family or a legally designated guardian is included in decision-making, or makes the decision as a surrogate decision-maker if legally required.

- Acts as an advocate for individuals with I/DD and their families when appropriate.

- Facilitates the individual with I/DD's self-determination in all healthcare settings.

- Refers the individual with I/DD to a qualified advocate when appropriate.

- Works to prevent and promptly respond to suspicion or evidence of abuse or exploitation, and reports the abuse to appropriate authorities.

- Identifies a surrogate for healthcare decisions in lieu of a formal guardianship process, when appropriate and in accordance with local or state statutes.

- Advocates for the individual with I/DD's self-determination when in conflict with the surrogate decision-maker.

- Assists in identifying the most appropriate living arrangements for the individual with I/DD in the least restrictive environment.

- Contributes to the educational program recommendations and advocates for the least restrictive environment to maximize the individual with I/DD's potential.

- Contributes to the life plan and advocates for the most appropriate employment situation. The nurse assists in identifying reasonable accommodations to maximize the individual with I/DD's performance and satisfaction with chosen employment.

- Serves as an advocate to ensure that individuals with I/DD have access to health care that provides continuity and is provided by a practitioner competent to manage the health concerns of individuals with I/DD.

- Facilitates the individual with I/DD's expression of sexuality in a manner that is consistent with the individual's native culture, religious upbringing, family values, and level of maturity, and provides counseling as appropriate. The nurse contributes to an environment that protects the individual with I/DD from sexual exploitation at home, school, work, and in the community.

- Assists in the referral process for local, state, regional, and federal assistance programs.

STANDARD 13. RESEARCH
The registered nurse who specializes in I/DD integrates research findings into practice.

Measurement Criteria

The registered nurse:

- Uses the best available evidence, including research findings, to guide practice decisions.

- Actively participates in research activities at various levels appropriate to the nurse's level of education and position. Such activities may include:

  - Identifying clinical problems specific to nursing research (patient care and nursing practice).

  - Participating in data collection (surveys, pilot projects, formal studies).

  - Participating in a formal committee or program.

  - Sharing research activities and findings with peers and others.

  - Conducting research.

  - Critically analyzing and interpreting research for application to practice.

  - Using research findings in the development of policies, procedures, and standards of practice in patient care.

  - Incorporating research as a basis for learning.

Additional Measurement Criteria for the Advanced Practice Registered Nurse

The advanced practice registered nurse:

- Contributes to nursing knowledge by conducting or synthesizing research that discovers, examines, and evaluates knowledge, theories, criteria, and creative approaches to improve healthcare practice.

- Formally disseminates research findings through activities such as presentations, publications, consultation, and journal clubs.

Additional Measurement Criteria for the Nursing Role Specialty

The registered nurse in a nursing role specialty:

- Contributes to nursing knowledge in the field of I/DD by conducting or synthesizing research that discovers, examines, and evaluates knowledge, theories, criteria, and creative approaches to improve healthcare practice and lives of individuals with I/DD.

- Participates in human subject protection activities as appropriate and is particularly cognizant of the vulnerability and exploitation of individuals with I/DD.

- Formally disseminates research findings through activities such as presentations, publications, consultation, interdisciplinary team meetings, and journal clubs.

Standard 14. Resource Utilization
The registered nurse specializing in I/DD considers factors related to safety, effectiveness, cost, and impact on practice in the planning and delivery of nursing services to individuals with I/DD.

Measurement Criteria
The registered nurse:

- Evaluates factors, such as safety, effectiveness, availability, cost and benefits, efficiencies, and impact on practice when choosing practice options that would result in the same expected outcome.

- Assists the individual with I/DD, family, or significant others in identifying and securing appropriate and available services to address health-related needs.

- Assigns or delegates tasks based on the needs and condition of the individual with I/DD, potential for hardship, stability of the individual with I/DD's condition, complexity of the task, and predictability of the outcome.

- Assists the individual with I/DD and family in becoming informed consumers about the options, costs, risks, and benefits of treatment and care.

Additional Measurement Criteria for the Advanced Practice Registered Nurse
The advanced practice registered nurse:

- Uses organizational and community resources to formulate interdisciplinary plans of care.

- Develops innovative solutions for patient care problems that address effective resource utilization and maintenance of quality.

- Develops evaluation strategies to demonstrate cost effectiveness, cost benefit, and efficiency factors associated with nursing practice.

Additional Measurement Criteria for the Nursing Role Specialty

The registered nurse in a nursing role specialty:

- Develops innovative solutions and applies strategies to obtain appropriate resources for nursing initiatives.

- Secures organizational resources to ensure a work environment conducive to completing the identified plan and outcomes.

- Develops evaluation methods to measure safety and effectiveness for interventions and outcomes.

- Promotes activities that assist others, as appropriate, in becoming informed about costs, risks, and benefits of care, or of the plan and solution.

Standard 15. Leadership
The nurse who specializes in I/DD provides leadership in the professional practice setting and the profession.

Measurement Criteria
The registered nurse:

- Engages in teamwork as a team player and a team builder.

- Works to create and maintain healthy work environments in local, regional, national, or international communities.

- Displays the ability to define a clear vision, the associated goals, and a plan to implement and measure progress.

- Demonstrates a commitment to continuous, lifelong learning for self and others.

- Teaches others to succeed by mentoring and other strategies.

- Exhibits creativity and flexibility through times of change.

- Demonstrates energy, excitement, and a passion for quality work.

- Willingly accepts mistakes by self and others, thereby creating a culture in which risk-taking is not only safe, but expected.

- Inspires loyalty through valuing of people as the most precious asset in an organization.

- Directs the coordination of care across settings and among caregivers, including oversight of licensed and unlicensed personnel, including direct care support professionals, in any assigned or delegated tasks.

- Serves in key roles in the work setting by participating on committees, councils, and administrative teams.

- Promotes advancement of the profession through participation in professional nursing and interdisciplinary organizations.

Additional Measurement Criteria for the Advanced Practice Registered Nurse

The advanced practice registered nurse:

- Works to influence decision-making bodies to improve the care of individuals with I/DD.

- Provides direction to enhance the effectiveness of the healthcare team.

- Initiates and revises protocols or guidelines to reflect evidence-based practice, to reflect accepted changes in care management, or to address emerging problems.

- Promotes communication of information and advancement of the profession through writing, publishing, and presentations for professional or lay audiences.

- Designs innovations to effect change in practice and improve health outcomes.

Additional Measurement Criteria for the Nursing Role Specialty

The registered nurse in a nursing role specialty:

- Works to influence decision-making bodies to improve patient care, health services, and policies as they affect individuals with I/DD.

- Promotes communication of information and advancement of the profession as it relates to nursing and the field of I/DD through writing, publishing, and presentations for professional or lay audiences.

- Designs innovations to effect change in practice and outcomes.

- Provides direction to enhance the effectiveness of the interdisciplinary team.

Glossary

Collaborative care. Care based on interdisciplinary problem-solving in which there is respect for the perspectives, abilities, knowledge, and experiences of each person who is involved in making decisions that affect an individual's health, education, or vocational goals and programs.

Comprehensive care. Care that integrates health (primary, secondary, and tertiary levels) and social/family support programs with educational or vocational services.

Coordinated care. Care that facilitates access to needed resources and services and promotes continuity of care among multiple providers and diverse service systems. Work is done collaboratively with the individual and family members to achieve mutually agreed upon goals. Timeliness, appropriateness, and completeness of care are central to this concept.

Cultural competence. Care that respects, honors, and incorporates beliefs, norms, attitudes, and life practices of individuals and their families.

Developmentally appropriate care. Care focused on the unique needs of individuals to promote the developmental skills and independence consistant with the individual's present functional abilities rather than chronological age.

Developmental screening. Assessing a person's global or specific domains of development for evidence of developmental deviation. The results of screening are not diagnostic, and if the results are suspicious they must be repeated within a short period. If developmental delay is suspected after repeated screening, the person should be referred for diagnosis and appropriate treatment and intervention.

Early intervention. The provision of health, social, and educational services in an interdisciplinary setting for children from birth to 3 years of age at risk for or diagnosed with I/DD.

Family-centered care. Care to individuals in need of special services (e.g. therapies, rehabilitation, adaptive equipment) that is provided within the context of their family. The strengths, individuality, and diversity of each family are acknowledged and valued. The cornerstone of family-centered care is a partnership between the family and the professionals.

Inclusion. Integration of all persons, regardless of special needs and disabilities or the environment (e.g. school, community, etc.), with typical peers in the least restrictive setting. Innovative programs geared to the individual's strengths and capabilities must be provided.

Individualized education plan (IEP). An annual educational program plan and goals that are jointly determined by the school teachers, therapists, school nurse, and parents of the school-aged child with I/DD and members of their support system. The IEP includes all developmental and academic testing results, the child's health status, and the child's strengths and weaknesses, as well as transition plans. This plan may include vocational goals beginning at age 14.

Individualized family service plan (IFSP). An annual family service plan that includes goals and interventions for the entire family of a child, birth to 3 years diagnosed with or at risk for I/DD. The IFSP includes the child's strengths and weaknesses, the results of developmental testing in all areas of adaptive living, family needs, the identification of community resources, and plans for transition to the school setting. This plan is devised by the interdisciplinary team and the parents of the child with I/DD and members of their support system.

Individualized plan for employment (IPE). An annual work or habilitation plan, usually completed for adults with I/DD, that includes goals and interventions as determined by the individual, their family, and the interdisciplinary team at the individual's place of employment or residence. The IPE includes all developmental, adaptive skill levels, habilitative training and skill levels, and the individual's strengths and weaknesses, which are summarized into a plan.

Individualized transition plan (ITP). An annual transition plan, to begin when the adolescent with I/DD reaches 14 to 16 years of age, which includes goals and interventions as determined by the individual, his or her family, and the interdisciplinary team for the transition to adulthood. The ITP includes the individual's health, developmental, adaptive skill levels, strengths and weaknesses, and goals for a successful transition into adulthood that incorporates all aspects of the individual's life.

Interdisciplinary team. A group of professionals with varied and specialized backgrounds who work with the individual and family to make decisions about all aspects of the individual with I/DD's life and includes health, education, and vocational needs. This planning should be person centered. The membership of the interdisciplinary team should be determined by the type of expertise needed to meet the individual's needs.

Least restrictive environment. Identification of the environment that offers the person with I/DD the least amount of restriction from carrying out their activities of daily living.

Normalization. Providing a supportive environment for persons with I/DD to make decisions regarding activities of daily living and to live as close as possible to the norms and patterns in the mainstream of the society in which they reside.

Nursing. The protection, promotion, and optimization of health and abilities, prevention of illness and injury, alleviation of suffering through the diagnosis and treatment of human response, and advocacy in the care of individuals, families, communities, and populations (ANA, 2003).

Person-centered (youth-centered) care. Care that is centered around the wishes of the individual with I/DD after the individual and their family are fully informed of the knowledge and options available in regards to their care.

Scope of practice. The art and science or the totality of the practice of nursing.

Standard. Authoritative statements by which the nursing profession describes responsibilities for which its practitioners are accountable. These standards reflect the values and priorities of the profession and provide direction for nursing practice and a framework for the evaluation of practice. Standards define the nursing profession's accountability to the public and the client outcomes for which nurses are responsible (ANA, 1991).

Standards of practice. Authoritative statements that encompass the minimal competency level of nursing care and involve the process of assessment, diagnosis, outcomes identification, planning, implementation, and evaluation.

Standards of professional performance. Authoritative statements that encompass the minimal competency level of professional performance and involve the functions of quality of practice, education, professional practice evaluation, collegiality, collaboration, ethics, research, resource utilization, and leadership.

References

Aggen, R. L., M. D. DeGennaro, L. Fox, J. E. Hahn, B. A. Logan, and L. VonFumetti. 1995. *Standards of developmental disabilities nursing practice.* Eugene, OR: Developmental Disabilities Nurses Association.

Aggen, R. L., and N. J. Moore. 1984. *Standards of nursing practice in mental retardation/developmental disabilities.* Albany: New York State Office of Mental Retardation and Developmental Disabilities.

American Nurses Association (ANA). 2004. *Nursing: Scope and standards of practice.* Washington, DC: nursesbooks.org.

———. 2003. *Nursing's social policy statement.* 2nd ed. Washington, DC: nursesbooks.org.

———. 2001. *Code of ethics for nurses with interpretive statements.* Washington, DC: American Nurses Publishing.

———. 1999. *Scope and standards of public health nursing practice.* Washington, DC:American Nurses Publishing.

———. 1991. *Standards of clinical nursing practice.* Washington, DC: American Nurses Publishing.

American Psychiatric Nurses Association, International Society of Psychiatric–Mental Health Nurses, and American Nurses Association. 2000. *Scope and standards of psychiatric-mental health nursing practice.* Washington, DC: American Nurses Publishing .

Asch, A. 2001. Disability, bioethics, and human rights. In *Handbook of disability studies,* ed. G. L. Albrecht, K. D. Seelman, and M. Bury. Thousand Oaks, CA: Sage.

Austin, J., M. Challela, C. Huber, W. Sciarillo, and C. Stade. 1987. *Standards for the clinical advanced practice registered nurse in developmental disabilities/handicapping conditions.* Washington, DC: American Association of University Affiliated Programs.

Burling, S. 2002. Penn hospital to limit its care in futile cases. *Philadelphia Inquirer*, November 4, p. A1.

Colorado Collective for Medical Decisions. 1999. *Neonatal guidelines*. Denver: Author.

Consensus Committee. 1993. *National standards of nursing practice for early intervention services.* Lexington: University of Kentucky, College of Nursing.

———. 1994. *Standards of nursing practice for the care of children and adolescents with special health and developmental needs*. Vienna, VA: National Maternal and Child Health Clearinghouse.

Developmental Disabilities Assistance and Bill of Rights Act of 2000. 2000. Pub L. No. 106-402, 114 Stat. 1678.

Haynes, U. 1968. *Guidelines for nursing standards in residential centers for the mentally retarded*. Washington, DC: United Cerebral Palsy Association.

Igoe, J. B., P. Green, H. Heim, M. Licata, G. P. MacDonough, and B. A. McHugh. 1980. *School nurses working with handicapped children*. Kansas City, MO: American Nurses Association.

International Society of Nurses in Genetics, Inc., and American Nurses Association. 1998. *Statement on the scope and standards of genetics clinical nursing practice*. Washington, DC: American Nurses Publishing.

Luckasson, R., S., et al. 2002. *Mental retardation: Definition, classification, and systems of supports.* 10th ed. Washington, DC: American Association on Mental Retardation.

National Association of School Nurses and American Nurses Association. 2001. *Scope and standards of professional school nursing practice.* Washington, DC: American Nurses Publishing.

Nerney, T. 2000. *This is freedom*. White paper delivered to AAMR 12th Annual Meeting, Washington, DC Retrieved December 8, 2003 from URL: http://www.aamr.org/Reading_Room/pdf/nerney_whitepaper.pdf

Nehring, W. M. 1999. *A history of nursing in the field of mental retardation and developmental disabilities.* Washington, DC: American Association on Mental Retardation.

———. 2003. The American experience. *Learning Disability Practice* 6, no. 3:20-2.

Nehring, W. M., S. P. Roth, D. Natvig, J. S. Morse, T. Savage, and M. Krajicek. 1998. *Statement on the scope and standards for the nurse who specializes in developmental disabilities and/or mental retardation.* Washington, DC: American Nurses Association and American Association on Mental Retardation.

Roth, S. P., and J. S. Morse, J. S., eds. 1994. *A life-span approach to nursing care for individuals with developmental disabilities.* Baltimore: Brookes.

Society of Pediatric Nurses and American Nurses Association. 2003. *Scope and standards of pediatric nursing practice.* Washington, DC: American Nurses Publishing.

U.S. Public Health Service. 2002. *Closing the gap: A national blueprint for improving the health of individuals with mental retardation.* Report of the Surgeon General's conference on health disparities and mental retardation. Washington, DC: Author.

Williams, G. 2001. Theorizing disability. In *Handbook of disability studies,* ed. G. L. Albrecht, K. D. Seelman, M. Bury. Thousand Oaks, CA: Sage.

Statement on the
Scope and Standards
for the Nurse
Who Specializes in
Developmental
Disabilities and/or
Mental Retardation

American Association on Mental Retardation

American Nurses Association

CONTENTS

PREFACE

In recent years, individuals with a developmental disability and/or mental retardation (hereafter referred to as DD and/or MR) and their families have been asked to work collaboratively with health care professionals in making decisions about health care. Family members have become more sophisticated in their collaboration with health care professionals to optimize the care and treatment given to the individual with DD and/or MR. This advocacy has arisen in tandem with a radically evolving health care system that may or may not optimize treatment options for all people. Therefore, in response to these changes, individuals with DD and/or MR and their families should be assured of safe and effective nursing care.

The American Nurses Association (ANA) has been the vanguard for nursing practice for the past century. The *Code for Nurses with Interpretive Statements* (ANA, 1985), the *Standards of Clinical Nursing Practice* (ANA, 1991), and *Nursing's Social Policy Statement* (ANA, 1995) are all documents produced by this organization which prescribe nursing standards. These documents are intended to provide the public with assurances of safe and competent nursing care. Along with these documents, specialty nursing organizations have worked with the ANA to publish specific standards of care and professional practice in their specialty. This document concerning the care of individuals with DD and/or MR is a revision of the *Standards for the Clinical Nurse Specialist in Developmental Disabilities/Handicapping Conditions* (Austin, Challela, Huber, Sciarillo, & Stade, 1987). This document has been revised (a) to capture the changing practice of nursing in this specialty (i.e., encompassing all levels of education, all system levels of care from the individual to public policy), (b) to emphasize the unique health care needs and characteristics of individuals of all ages with DD and/or MR, and (c) to incorporate the ANA standards mentioned above (ANA, 1985; 1991; 1995). This document should also be used in conjunction with other standards of care and professional performance developed by other specialty nursing groups [e.g., *Statement on the Scope and Standards of Pediatric Clinical Nursing Practice* (Society of Pediatric Nurses, 1996); *Standards of Nursing Practice for the Care of Children and Adolescents with Special Health and Developmental Needs* (Consensus Committee and the Maternal-

Child Health Bureau, 1994); *Standards of Community Health Nursing Practice* (ANA, 1986); *Standards of Psychiatric-Mental Health Clinical Nursing Practice* (ANA, 1994b)].

Standards of care and professional performance are also being written by specialty groups to represent the current level of knowledge and practice in that specialty. They are dynamic in nature and subject to change over time. Standards of care and professional performance provide guidelines by which a nurse's practice can be measured and evaluated. They can also be used for peer review, in research to validate nursing practice, for utilization review and reimbursement designations, and in program and policy development. Each standard of care and professional performance listed in this document has been standardized by the ANA (ANA, 1994a). The measurement criteria have been developed by this Task Force to represent quality care and performance in the nursing care of individuals with DD and/or MR.

STATEMENT ON THE SCOPE OF PRACTICE FOR THE NURSE WHO SPECIALIZES IN DEVELOPMENTAL DISABILITIES AND/OR MENTAL RETARDATION (DD and/or MR)

Nursing for people with DD and/or MR focuses on assisting individuals with DD and/or MR to attain and maintain optimal wellness across the life span. These individuals experience disorders that reflect a variety of health, cognitive, communication, social adaptation, sensory, perceptual, gross motor, and fine motor strengths and limitations. They are manifested with varying intensity over time and have significant impact on the family as well as the individual (Morse, 1994).

Developmental disability is a broad term that refers to a wide variety of mental and/or physical conditions that interfere with the ability of an individual to function effectively in daily living. Environmental deprivation as well as biological limitations may contribute to the individual's impairment. A developmental disability is present before the age of 22 years and generally continues throughout life (U.S. House of Representatives, 1978; Morse, 1994). The definition of mental retardation is similar to that of developmental disability except that it is manifested prior to the age of 18 years (Luckasson, Coulter, Polloway, Reiss, Schalock, Snell, Spitalnik, & Stark, 1992).

The nursing needs of individuals with DD and/or MR are unique and require the skills of the professional nurse in interdisciplinary team settings. These settings include large public and private agencies, small community-based facilities, and foster and biological homes. They also include services provided through hospitals, communities, organizations, and schools. The nurse's understanding of the interaction among physical, affective, and cognitive systems prepares him or her to contribute to the interdisciplinary process intended to improve the quality of life for individuals with DD and/or MR and their families (Steadham & Frank, 1993).

Nurses play an important role in the promotion of health, wellness, and normalization in the delivery of nursing services to individuals with DD and/or MR. Three key components in this role are education, prevention, and support. Nurses actively provide case-finding, education, care coordination, and direct nursing services on primary, secondary, and tertiary prevention levels across the life span to individuals with DD and/or MR and their families. This care results in a holistic approach to the integration of health care services in habilitation (the process by which individuals develop new skills and abilities).

Currently, nurses in DD and/or MR are involved through their practice and advocacy in a number of issues predominant in the field. These issues include cultural concerns, early assessment and identification in the birth-to-three-years population, inclusion in the school setting, adult health care, and genetics. As nurses care for persons with DD and/or MR and their families from diverse backgrounds, culturally competent methods of communication, care, and intervention must be developed and evaluated. Nurses play a key role in the management of the school-aged child with DD and/or MR. Moreover, as persons with DD and/or MR are living longer, the need to define adult and older adult health care and provide appropriate interventions is imperative for safe and effective nursing care. New discoveries in identifying the human genome have created vast opportunities for nurses to improve case-finding, education, prevention of primary and secondary disease conditions, care coordination, and evaluation.

Furthermore, nursing care of individuals with DD and/or MR, provided across the life span, in the continuum from primary to tertiary prevention may be defined as those activities which include—

- *health promotion*: encouraging healthy patterns of living;
- *health support*: developing new behaviors or modifying existing stressors that have the potential to interfere with health and development; and
- *health restoration*: modifying the negative impact of developmental disabilities upon the individual, family, and/or community (Brown & Roth, 1994).

At each level of prevention, nurses who specialize in the care of individuals with DD and/or MR provide services which incorporate the following functions:

- *assessment:* assessing the health of the community's residents and the adequacy of community resources to prevent

DD and/or MR and to support individuals with DD and/or MR and their families;

- *policy development and implementation*: using data gathered through assessment to develop and advocate for public policies that support individuals with DD and/or MR and their families; and
- *assurance*: evaluating and improving the availability, accessibility, effectiveness, and quality of services available through monitoring, evaluation, and quality assurance activities (Washington State Task Force, 1993).

The nurse's practice in DD and/or MR is both independent and collaborative. Under professional licensure, the nurse's independent responsibility is screening, nursing diagnosis, and the care of human responses to health, illness, and adverse circumstances that threaten independence and individual well-being, and the evaluation of individual and family outcomes (ANA, 1995). Collaborative practice is based upon—

- mutual trust;
- mutual respect for cultural diversity;
- mutual respect for the strengths, interests, and needs of individuals with DD and/or MR and their families;
- mutual respect for the skills and knowledge of other disciplines;
- mutual agreement upon goals; and
- shared planning, decision-making, and joint responsibility for follow-through actions, solutions, and evaluation of outcomes (Brandt, 1993).

Therefore, the guiding principles for nurses to provide a continuum of services to individuals with DD and/or MR across the life span are (a) collaborative care, (b) comprehensive care, (c) coordinated care, (d) culturally competent care, (e) developmentally appropriate care, (f) family-centered care, and (g) inclusive care.

Guiding Principles

The nursing care of individuals with developmental disabilities and mental retardation across the life span is based upon seven guiding principles:

Collaborative Care: Care based on interdisciplinary problem solving in which there is respect for the perspectives, abilities, knowledge, and experiences of each person who is involved in making decisions that affect an individual's health, education, and/or vocational goals and programs.

Comprehensive Care: Care that integrates health (primary, secondary, and tertiary levels) and social/family support programs with educational or vocational services.

Coordinated Care: Care that facilitates access to needed resources and services and promotes continuity of care among multiple providers and diverse service systems. Work is done collaboratively with the individual and/or family members to achieve mutually agreed-upon goals. The timeliness, appropriateness, and completeness of care are central to this concept.

Culturally Competent Care: Care that respects, honors, and incorporates beliefs, norms, attitudes, and life practices of individuals and their families congruent with their values and practices.

Developmentally Appropriate Care: Care focused on the unique needs of individuals to promote the developmental skills and independence congruent with the individual's present functional abilities rather than chronological age.

Family-Centered Care: A recognition that care to individuals in need of special services (e.g., therapies, rehabilitation, adaptive equipment) can best be provided within the context of his or her family. The strengths, individuality, and diversity of each family are acknowledged and valued. The cornerstone of family-centered care is a partnership between the family and the professionals. In the absence of a family, care is client-centered.

Inclusive Care: Regardless of the environment (e.g., school, community, etc.), all persons, regardless of special needs or disabilities, are to be included or integrated with typical peers in the least restrictive setting. Programs geared to the individual's strengths and capabilities must be provided.

DESCRIPTION OF NURSING IN DEVELOPMENTAL DISABILITIES AND/OR MENTAL RETARDATION (DD and/or MR)

Nursing in DD and/or MR is the care of persons of all ages with DD and/or MR and their families across a variety of health care, educational, and residential settings. The nurse who practices in this specialty may serve in several capacities, including (a) clinician, (b) teacher, (c) interdisciplinary team member, (d) case manager, (e) advocate, (f) counselor, (g) consultant, (h) administrator, and (i) researcher (Feeg, 1994). Nurses who specialize in DD and/or MR have a broad range of concerns in providing holistic care to individuals, families, and communities (see Figure 1).

Figure 1. The Phenomena of Concern for Nurses Who Specialize in DD and/or MR

Individuals

- Unique anatomical, physiological, and psychological differences depending on diagnosis (e.g., genetic syndromes, congenital defects, physical deformities)
- Developmental interventions based on functional rather than chronological age
- Prevention of secondary impairments
- Adequate and appropriate primary health care and immunizations based on chronological age
- Appropriate management of acute and chronic illnesses
- Consistent collaboration with the individual regarding management of health care
- Health care teaching at the individual's developmental level
- Management of psychosocial concerns
- Developing, implementing, and evaluating the Individualized Family Service Plan (IFSP), the Individualized Education Plan (IEP), the Individualized Health Plan (IHP), or the Individualized Habilitation Plan (IHP) with the interdisciplinary team
- Advocacy
- Legal issues/concerns

continued on next page

Family

- Family-centered approach that is respectful of cultural and socioeconomic differences
- Consistent collaboration with family members regarding health promotion and management of health care and habilitation
- Advocacy
- Sensitivity to family concerns that support quality of life for persons with DD and/or MR

Community

- Case management across the person's life span
- Keeping abreast of advances in nursing and the other disciplines involved in the care of persons with DD and/or MR
- Economic and political changes and their influence on financial status of the family (e.g., changes in Supplemental Security Income policy)
- Staying informed of political and policy changes and being able to translate these changes to the individual and their family

ETHICS FOR THE NURSE WHO SPECIALIZES IN DEVELOPMENTAL DISABILITIES AND/OR MENTAL RETARDATION (DD and/or MR)

Understanding ethical principles plays an important role in the nursing of individuals with DD and/or MR. These individuals have a common characteristic as, to some degree, they are dependent. They require assistance from other persons ranging from supervision in their home and work environment to total dependency for activities of daily living. That dependency adds to the moral obligation society has to those individuals with DD and/or MR. Nurses have a distinct obligation to advocate and protect the interests of vulnerable patients/clients.

Parents act as their child's advocate and surrogate decision-maker. However, determining the best interests of the child is not always the exclusive purview of the parents. The 1982 case of Baby Doe challenged parental autonomy in the decision to forego life-sustaining treatment for an infant with Down's syndrome and duodenal atresia. Several years later, health care providers now work collaboratively with parents to assist them in their decisions regarding life-sustaining treatment for their children with DD and/or MR.

In adult decision-making, an adult is presumed to be competent unless evidence demonstrating incompetence to make a particular decision is presented to a court of law and "incompetence" is established. A guardian may be appointed to make decisions regarding person and property in the event an individual is declared legally incompetent. In health care decisions, the guardian is expected to use the *best interest* standard rather than *substituted judgment*.[1] The substituted judgment standard is based on the previously declared wishes of the person who was formerly competent but now lacks decisional capacity. Persons with DD and/or MR may never become competent to make health care

---

[1] President's Commission for the Study of Ethical Problems in Medicine and Biomedical and Behavioral Research (1983). *Deciding to Forego Life-Sustaining Treatment*. Washington, DC: U.S. Government Printing Office.

decisions. Whereas the law proposes clear boundaries between competent and incompetent, nurses often appreciate subtle "gray" areas in which persons with DD and/or MR should have a voice in health care decisions. The standards in this publication are intended to guide nurses in advocating for persons with DD and/or MR and in facilitating ethical decision-making with them as well as on their behalf.

SCOPE OF NURSING PRACTICE FOR THE NURSE WHO SPECIALIZES IN DEVELOPMENTAL DISABILITIES AND/OR MENTAL RETARDATION (DD and/or MR)

These standards outline levels of professional nursing practice to be attained by the nurse who specializes in DD and/or MR. These standards reflect two practice levels: the generalist nurse and the advanced practice nurse. The advanced practice nurse is a specialist, prepared at the graduate level. In the absence of the advanced practice nurse, the generalist assumes many, but not all, of the aspects of the more comprehensive role of the specialist. The authors of these Standards recommend that the generalist level include nurses who are educationally prepared at the baccalaureate level. All nurses working in the field of DD and/or MR are encouraged to use these Standards as a guide in providing care.

Basic Level

The nurse generalist who specializes in DD and/or MR provides care to individuals, families, and groups in a wide range of care settings with an understanding of the concepts and strategies of nursing practice in this area. The generalist participates in the implementation of individual and family assessment and in the planning, implementation, and evaluation of their health and health services. The generalist may serve as a case manager with individuals with DD and/or MR who have less complex needs, if an advanced practice nurse is not available. The generalist uses the advanced practice nurse in DD and/or MR as a resource. If no advanced practice nurse is available in the practice setting, advanced practice nurses who can serve as consultants may be available through the Nursing Division of the American Association on Mental Retardation or through the University Affiliated Programs (UAPs).

Advanced Level

The master's or doctorally prepared nurse who specializes in DD and/or MR is an advanced practice nurse or specialist who is capable of, and has the authority to, perform all of the functions of the generalist with a more independent and sophisticated theoretical and clinical focus. The master's prepared nurse may be clinically employed in the role of clinical nurse specialist, nurse consultant, nurse practitioner, nurse educator, or nurse administrator. The doctorally prepared nurse may function in a clinical, education, administration, consultation, or research role. In addition, the advanced practice nurse possesses substantial experience with individuals with DD and/or MR, their families, and community resources; skill in the formulation and implementation of social policy and legislation affecting persons with DD and/or MR; ability to plan, implement, and evaluate programs designed to serve individuals with DD and/or MR and their families; and the ability to conduct research. These skills are based upon knowledge of specific DD and/or MR, including their epidemiology, etiology, and demographics. The advanced practice nurse understands the use of technology for persons with DD and/or MR as well as the impact of social, psychological, educational, cultural, and religious values on individuals, their families, and communities. The advanced practice nurse in DD and/or MR must be knowledgeable about cost containment, legislation, and policy planning to provide preventive, supportive, and restorative care to individuals with DD and/or MR across the life span in a wide variety of settings.

The advanced practice nurse is prepared to engage in interdisciplinary assessments, interventions, and teaching with an emphasis on individual and family-centered services delivered within a community context. The advanced practice nurse is also able to serve as a case manager and interdisciplinary team leader, and to identify and develop a program of research relevant to the practice of nursing in DD and/or MR. This document emphasizes the development and maintenance of skills necessary to promote positive health outcomes for the entire population of individuals with DD and/or MR and does not focus on a particular clinical diagnosis.

STANDARDS OF PRACTICE FOR THE NURSE WHO SPECIALIZES IN DEVELOPMENTAL DISABILITIES AND/OR MENTAL RETARDATION (DD and/or MR)

As stated before, these standards have been revised to reflect the changing nature of health care and the field of DD and/or MR. Recent political influences and policy changes have left individuals with DD and/or MR and their families concerned about how they will receive optimal quality health care across time. The discipline of nursing must also assure the public that its practitioners are able to provide competent care to individuals with DD and/or MR. Thus, these standards are reflective of the values and responsibilities of nurses in this specialty.

These standards are written in a measurable format under the guidelines established by the ANA (1991). They provide direction for those nurses specializing in this field and provide a foundation for the evaluation of nursing practice. These standards apply to both the generalist and advanced practice nurse in DD and/or MR. They apply to the nursing care of persons with DD and/or MR of all ages, cultures, socioeconomic backgrounds, and medical diagnoses. Furthermore, these standards apply to any health care, education, residential, or community setting where individuals with DD and/or MR might be found.

The "Standards of Care" reflect many components of the nursing process, including assessment, diagnosis, outcome identification, planning, implementation, and evaluation. This process of fact-finding, decision-making, action, and evaluation should take place in any situation involving a person with DD and/or MR. Both the generalist and advanced practice nurse will use this process in his or her practice. Each measurement criterion implies a minimally competent level of practice and, unless otherwise stated, applies to both the nurse generalist and the nurse specialist.

The "Standards of Professional Performance" reflect the role functions of nursing: quality of care, performance appraisal, education, collegiality, ethics, collaboration, research, and resource utilization. Each of these areas is equally important in the care of persons with DD and/or MR as they are in any other specialty of nursing. How they are implemented and evaluated depends on the level of education, state nursing practice laws, employment setting, and position. For example, in the first standard, "Quality of Care," the measurement criteria have been divided into administrative and direct service activities. Each measurement criterion implies a minimally competent level of practice and, unless otherwise stated, applies to both the nurse generalist and the nurse specialist.

Standards of practice for any specialty must be dynamic and reflective of the current state of knowledge and practice. Standards of practice should be assessed along with other measures (e.g., educational degrees) and documents [e.g., *Nursing's Social Policy Statement* (ANA, 1995)], and state nursing practice acts which provide guidelines for evaluating nursing practice. Standards of practice can be used (a) in practice for the development of job position descriptions, performance evaluations, reimbursement ratings determinations, and utilization review; (b) in the development and validation of nursing theory and/or theory from related disciplines in relation to DD and/or MR; (c) in the development and testing of research questions; (d) in the development, implementation, and evaluation of instruction to individuals and families by nurses or educational programs for groups of nurses, health care professionals, individuals with DD and/or MR, their families, or the public; and (e) in the development of policy related to service, practice, and federal financing programs. The authors welcome any comments or suggestions regarding these standards for future revisions.

KEY TERMS

Additional terms are found in the glossary at the end of the Standards.

Case Management—A delivery system that focuses on outcomes by providing coordination of health care services and resources to meet the needs of a person with DD and/or MR by decreasing fragmentation, enhancing the person's quality of life, and containing costs. Case management also involves the provision of information to family members and to agencies regarding the person across settings and time (ANA, 1986; Huber, 1996).

Developmental Disabilities—A severe, chronic disability of a person which is attributable to a mental or physical impairment or a combination of mental and physical impairment; is manifested before the person attains 22 years of age; is likely to continue indefinitely; results in substantial limitations in three or more of the following areas of major life activity: self-care, receptive and expressive language, learning, mobility, self-direction, capacity for independent living, and economic sufficiency; reflects the person's need for a combination and sequence of special, interdisciplinary or generic care, treatment, or the services which are of life-long or extended duration and are individually planned and coordinated (U.S. House of Representatives, 1978, pp. 51-52).

Developmental Screening—Refers to the process of generally assessing a person's global or specific domains of development for evidence of delays in performance of key tasks. The results of screening are not diagnostic and if the results are suspicious, then they must be repeated within a short period of time. If developmental delay is suspected after the repeated screening, the person should be referred for diagnosis and appropriate treatment and intervention.

Early Intervention—The provision of health, social, and educational services in an interdisciplinary or transdisciplinary setting for children birth-to-three years of age at-risk for and/or with DD and/or MR (Russell & Free, 1994).

Family—A group of people who are either biologically related or a network of individuals who influence and support each other.

Individualized Educational Plan (IEP)—An annual educational program plan and goals that are jointly determined by the school teachers, therapists, school nurse, and parents of the school-aged child with DD and/or MR and members of their support system. The IEP should include all developmental and academic assessment results, the child's health status, and the child's strengths and weaknesses, as well as transition plans. This plan should include vocational goals beginning in the junior high school years.

Individualized Family Service Plan (IFSP)—An annual family service plan that includes goals and interventions for the entire family of a child, birth-to-three years, with DD and/or MR. The IFSP should include the child's strengths and weaknesses; the results of developmental assessments in all areas of adaptive living; identification of family concerns, priorities, and resources; identification of community resources; and plans for transition to the school setting. This plan should be devised by the parents of the child with DD and/or MR and members of their support system, including any professionals providing care for or on behalf of the child (Russell & Free, 1994).

Individualized Habilitation Plan (IHP)—An annual habilitation plan, usually completed for adults with DD and/or MR, that includes goals and interventions as determined by the individual, his or her family, and the interdisciplinary team at the individual's place of employment and/or residence. The IHP should include all developmental and adaptive skill levels, health status, habilitative training and skill levels, and the individual's strengths and weaknesses, which are summarized into the plan.

Individualized Health Plan—An annual health plan that is individualized by the interdisciplinary team and most often completed by the health care professionals on the team. These plans are often included in school settings and reflect short- and long-term objectives related to the person's primary and secondary health conditions.

Interdisciplinary Team (IDT)—A group of professional and lay people with varied and specialized backgrounds who assist the individual and/or family in making decisions about the health, educational, social, habilitative, and/or vocational needs of a person with DD and/or MR. The membership of the IDT should be determined by the type of expertise needed to meet the individual's needs and with the individual's or family's consent about the membership. The person with DD and/or MR and the family members are integral parts of the IDT (Natvig, 1996).

Least Restrictive Environment—Identification of the environment that offers the person with DD and/or MR the least amount of restriction to carrying out their activities of daily living.

Mental Retardation—An important subcategory of developmental disabilities that refers to substantial limitations in present functioning. It is characterized by significantly subaverage intellectual functioning, existing concurrently with related limitations in two or more of the following applicable adaptive skills areas: communication, self-care, home living, social skills, community use, self-direction, health and safety, functional academics, leisure, and work. Mental retardation manifests before age 18 (Luckasson, et al., 1992).

Normalization—Providing a supportive environment for persons with DD and/or MR to make decisions regarding activities of daily living. Assisting persons to live as close as possible to the norms and patterns in the mainstream of the society in which they reside.

STANDARDS OF CARE

Standard I. Assessment

The nurse who specializes in DD and/or MR collects data relevant to persons with DD and/or MR.

Measurement Criteria

INDIVIDUAL AND FAMILY

1. The **nurse generalist** systematically collects data about the individual and his or her family, through observation, interviewing, and use of screening and assessment tools. Diagnostic tests may be used as part of the assessment process if the nurse has specific training in that area.

2. The nurse prioritizes the data to be collected according to the individual's immediate condition, needs, concerns, priorities, strengths, and/or the purpose of the information needed.

3. The nurse validates data collected by sharing findings with the individual, family, or other members of the interdisciplinary team.

4. The nurse collects health-related data in the following areas:

   a. Health histories include but are not limited to—
      - family member's health and background
      - prenatal and pregnancy history
      - genetic studies
      - special serum screenings (e.g., cystic fibrosis, Tay-Sachs, sickle-cell disease, etc.)
      - patterns of growth and development
      - health patterns, illnesses, and injuries
      - nutritional needs and metabolic functioning
      - problems or concerns with sexual or reproductive function

- rest and sleep patterns
- elimination patterns including bowel and bladder functioning
- family, social, cultural, and community support systems
- health beliefs and practices
- strengths and competencies that can be used to promote health
- economic, political, legal, and environmental factors affecting health
- medication history differentiating between prescription and over-the-counter medications (including medications for behavior control and/or mental health conditions).

   b. Physical status

   c. Mental and emotional status

   d. Nutritional status

   e. Factors that affect activity, exercise, self-help, and recreational or vocational aspirations such as neuromuscular, cardiovascular, communication, respiratory, and developmental functioning

   f. Risk factors that may affect health.

5. The nurse records data in a timely, standardized, systematic, and concise manner.

6. The **nurse specialist** designs, manages, and evaluates the data collection system and coordinates his or her data collection system with other data sources.

7. The **nurse specialist** serves as a consultant to the **nurse generalist** and others in the interdisciplinary team in the use of the data collection system.

COMMUNITY

1. The **nurse generalist**, in collaboration with the **nurse specialist** and in partnership with key informants, collects community data related to the individual with DD and/or MR. This includes but is not limited to—

- vital statistics
- demographics
- community dynamics
- socioeconomic, cultural, and environmental chara-
teristics
- community resources.

2. The **nurse specialist** plans, implements, and evaluates data collection procedures, and makes decisions about advanced methodologies, such as surveys, sampling techniques, and the need for instrument development to obtain necessary information.

3. The **nurse specialist** establishes working relationships with community leaders who can influence quality of life for individuals with DD and/or MR.

Standard II. Diagnosis

The nurse who specializes in DD and/or MR analyzes the assessment data in determining nursing diagnoses.

Measurement Criteria

INDIVIDUAL AND FAMILY

1. The **nurse generalist**, in partnership with the individual and family, organizes, categorizes, interprets, and analyzes collected data to formulate nursing diagnoses.

2. Diagnoses and potential problem statements are derived from the assessment data.

3. Diagnoses reflect the strengths, priorities, needs, and concerns of individuals and families.

4. The nurse reviews and revises nursing diagnoses as new assessment information is obtained.

5. The **nurse specialist** serves as a consultant to the **nurse generalist** in formulation of nursing diagnoses as needed.

COMMUNITY

1. The **nurse specialist**, in collaboration with the **nurse generalist** and in partnership with the community, organizes, categorizes, interprets, and analyzes data to formulate nursing diagnoses or potential problem statements regarding—
   - accessibility and availability of services
   - barriers to adequate health care for individuals with DD and/or MR
   - specific populations at risk for DD and/or MR
   - health promotion needs for specific populations
   - environmental hazards that may affect health.

2. Diagnoses and potential problem statements are derived from the assessment data.

3. Diagnoses reflect the strengths, priorities, needs, and concerns of the community.

Standard III. Outcome Identification

The nurse who specializes in DD and/or MR assists the client in identifying expected outcomes individualized to the client, family, or community.

Measurement Criteria

INDIVIDUAL AND FAMILY

1. The **nurse generalist**, in partnership with the individual and family, formulates a plan of care with specific priorities and outcome measures.

2. Expected outcomes address needs revealed from assessment data.

3. Expected outcomes are congruent with the individual's present and potential capabilities and reflect his or her health and level of functioning.

4. Expected outcomes are documented in measurable terms and include a time frame for completion.

5. Expected outcomes are formulated by the nurse and individual, and the family, significant others, and the interdisciplinary team, when necessary.

6. Expected outcomes are focused on the individual, and are therapeutically sound, attainable, and cost-effective.

7. Expected outcomes reflect current scientific knowledge in DD and/or MR.

COMMUNITY

1. The **nurse specialist**, in collaboration with the **nurse generalist** and in partnership with the community, formulates a plan with specific priorities and outcome measures.

2. Expected outcomes are derived from nursing diagnoses and potential problem statements.

3. Expected outcomes are realistic in relation to the community's present and potential capabilities.

4. Expected outcomes are documented in measurable terms and include a time frame for completion.

5. Expected outcomes are attainable and cost-effective.

6. Expected outcomes reflect current scientific knowledge on service provision in DD and/or MR.

Standard IV. Planning

The nurse develops a plan that prescribes interventions to attain expected outcomes.

Measurement Criteria

INDIVIDUAL AND FAMILY

1. The **nurse generalist**, in partnership with the individual and family, devises plans that are based on identified nursing diagnoses, problems, conditions, or needs and that build on individual and/or family strengths.

2. Plans are developed in collaboration with the individual, family, significant others, and the interdisciplinary team, when appropriate.

3. Plans reflect relevant theoretical concepts and research findings.

4. Plans include prioritized, measurable goals, behavioral objectives with expected dates of accomplishment, and outcomes that are collaboratively established by the individual, family, and interdisciplinary team.

5. Plans identify a sequence of actions for achieving the goals and objectives.

6. Plans identify actions necessary to assure continuity of care where appropriate.

7. Resources necessary to accomplish the plan are identified.

8. Plans include a cost-benefit analysis.

9. Plans show evidence of revision as goals and objectives are achieved or modified.

10. The **nurse specialist** is used as a consultant to the **nurse generalist** in plan development, priority setting, and identification of resources, as needed.

COMMUNITY

1. The **nurse specialist**, in collaboration with the **nurse generalist** and in partnership with the community, devises community-focused plans that are based on identified problems, conditions, or needs and that build on the strengths of the community.

2. Plans reflect relevant theoretical concepts and research findings.

3. Plans include measurable goals and behavioral objectives with expected dates of accomplishment.

4. Plans identify a sequence of actions for achieving the goals and objectives.

5. Plans ensure continuity of care and minimize or eliminate gaps and overlaps in services.

6. Plans include the resources necessary to accomplish the plan.

7. Plans include a cost-benefit analysis.

8. Plans show evidence of revision as goals and objectives are achieved or modified.

Standard V. Implementation

The nurse who specializes in DD and/or MR implements interventions identified in the plan of care.

Measurement Criteria

INDIVIDUAL AND FAMILY

1. The **nurse generalist**, with the participation of the individual and family, implements interventions identified in the plan of care.

2. Interventions are within the scope of accepted nursing practice.

3. Nursing interventions address primary, secondary, and tertiary prevention strategies.

4. Interventions are performed in a safe, ethical, and appropriate manner.

5. Interventions are documented in a timely and appropriate manner.

6. The nurse serves as a coordinator of health services and as an advocate for the individual and family in achieving health goals.

7. The nurse collaborates with other members of the interdisciplinary team in implementing the plan of care.

8. The nurse makes referrals to other disciplines as needed.

9. The nurse supervises ancillary and unlicensed personnel who provide health care to families and individuals.

10. The nurse keeps the individual and family informed about their health status and the health care resources that are available.

11. The nurse teaches the individual and family self-care concepts and skills, and assists in modifying the environment to encourage their use.

12. The nurse reviews and revises interventions based on individual and family response.

COMMUNITY

1. The **nurse specialist** works in collaboration with the **nurse generalist** and other health care providers, community leaders, and other community organizations to help implement programs and develop resources necessary to meet identified needs.

2. Nursing interventions address primary, secondary, and tertiary prevention strategies.

3. The nurse assists in disseminating information about services and resources which are culturally and linguistically appropriate and are available to meet the health needs of individuals with DD and/or MR.

4. The **nurse specialist** serves as a resource to community leaders and agencies about the health care needs of individuals with DD and/or MR.

5. The **nurse specialist** formulates and influences health and social policies that affect individuals with DD and/or MR.

Standard VI. Evaluation

The nurse who specializes in DD and/or MR evaluates the client's, family's, and community's progress toward attainment of outcomes.

Measurement Criteria

INDIVIDUAL AND FAMILY

1. The **nurse generalist** plans for the ongoing, timely, and comprehensive evaluation of the outcomes of the interventions.

2. The nurse uses baseline and current data in measuring progress toward achievement of outcomes.

3. The nurse validates observations, insights, and new data with the individual, family, and other members of the interdisciplinary team.

4. The nurse, in partnership with the individual and the family, revises priorities, goals, and interventions to reflect the results of the evaluation process.

5. The nurse clearly documents evaluation results and revisions to the plan.

6. The nurse participates in the evaluation of the plan through record audit and other methods of peer review.

7. The **nurse specialist** serves as a consultant to the **nurse generalist** in evaluating the impact of the interventions with the individual and his or her family.

COMMUNITY

1. The **nurse generalist**, in collaboration with the **nurse specialist**, evaluates community responses to interventions.

2. The **nurse specialist** uses baseline and current data in measuring progress toward the achievement of outcomes.

3. The **nurse specialist** validates observations, insights, and new data with colleagues and community members.

4. The **nurse specialist**, in partnership with the community, revises priorities, goals, and interventions to reflect the results of the evaluation process.

5. The **nurse specialist** clearly documents evaluation results and revisions to the plan.

6. The **nurse specialist** conducts program evaluation in structure, process, and outcomes of health care that may include the following components:
   a. Cost-benefit analysis
   b. Documentation system
   c. Quality of interventions
   d. Immediate and long-term outcomes, both intended and unintended.

7. The **nurse specialist** communicates the results of program evaluation to other program planners and decision-makers.

8. The **nurse specialist** conducts evaluation research with consultation as needed.

9. Results of program evaluation are used in making future program decisions.

10. Evaluation processes and results are disseminated in a manner that contributes to the effectiveness of nursing actions, policy formation and evaluation, and research.

STANDARDS OF PROFESSIONAL PERFORMANCE

Standard I. Quality of Care

The nurse systematically evaluates the quality and effectiveness of nursing practice involving individuals with DD and/or MR.

Measurement Criteria

ADMINISTRATIVE ACTIVITIES

1. The nurse administrator establishes appropriate quality indicators and risk management implications for organizations serving individuals with DD and/or MR.

2. The nurse administrator collaborates with other members of the organization's management team to ensure that health care practices are emphasized and implemented throughout the organization serving individuals with DD and/or MR.

3. The nurse administrator analyzes how to positively influence nurse recruitment, job satisfaction, performance appraisal, discipline, and retention of nurses working with individuals with DD and/or MR.

4. The nurse administrator develops or participates in quality improvement programs to ensure that high-quality services are delivered in a consistent and cost-effective manner.

5. The nurse administrator evaluates the effectiveness and efficiency of nursing care for individuals with DD and/or MR in terms of client and cost outcomes.

6. The nurse administrator analyzes the manner in which standards of practice can be implemented into organizational systems for case management, referral, and follow-up to ensure continuity of care.

7. The nurse administrator develops policies, procedures, and service delivery strategies to improve nursing practice and client outcomes.

8. The nurse administrator ensures that adequate numbers of registered nurses and care providers are employed to support quality care.

9. The nurse administrator ensures that the agency's policies for delegation of nursing tasks are in accordance with the state's nurse practice act.

10. The nurse administrator develops adequate, appropriate, and ongoing in-service education and ensures that it is available for nurses and unlicensed personnel.

11. The nurse administrator encourages nurses to practice in accordance with the *Statement on the Scope and Standards for the Nurse Who Specializes in DD and/or MR* and other appropriate guidelines.

DIRECT CARE PROVIDER SERVICES

1. The nurse working with individuals with DD and/or MR collaborates with other providers in evaluating clinical practice, client outcomes, and systems of care.

2. The nurse working with individuals with DD and/or MR and their families evaluates nursing care delegated to other professionals, unlicensed assistive personnel, or the family and documents the effect of delegation on health outcomes.

3. The nurse participates in professional organizations which strive to improve the quality of nursing care and other services provided to individuals and families involved with DD and/or MR.

4. The nurse participates in or provides leadership to local, state, or national efforts to establish legislation, regula-

tion/policy, and service delivery systems that enable individuals and families involved with developmental disabilities to receive quality health care that is accessible and cost-effective.

Standard II. Performance Appraisal

The nurse evaluates his or her own nursing practice in relation to professional practice standards and relevant statutes and regulations.

Measurement Criteria

1. The nurse periodically evaluates individual, collaborative, or delegated practice in relationship to standards established by the profession and relevant statutes and regulations.

2. The nurse contributes to the performance appraisal process by identifying areas of strength as well as areas for professional/practice development.

3. The nurse initiates and participates in the peer review process.

4. The nurse incorporates appropriate changes in his or her own practice suggested by self-evaluation, evaluation by clients and families, peer evaluation, and professional development activities.

Standard III. Education

The nurse working with individuals with DD and/or MR acquires and maintains current knowledge in nursing practice to effectively implement standards for practice.

Measurement Criteria

1. The nurse identifies theory and specialized content relevant to the practice of nursing in DD and/or MR.

2. The nurse in the field of DD and/or MR develops a conceptual framework for practice based on relevant theories and specialized content, applying it to all phases of nursing practice (screening, assessment, planning, intervention, evaluation, and referral) and testing its effectiveness in predicting, understanding, and caring for individuals with DD and/or MR and their families.

3. The nurse engages in educational activities to improve clinical knowledge and skills, enhance role performance, and increase understanding of professional issues.

4. The nurse incorporates updated clinical knowledge and skills into his or her practice.

5. The nurse seeks certification or credentialing as appropriate for his or her practice area.

6. The nurse participates in professional development programs such as continuing education, conventions, and formal academic study to increase knowledge and skills pertinent to nursing practice for individuals with DD and/or MR.

7. The nurse shares his or her clinical and/or research expertise through speaking engagements, writing for refereed journals and/or books, and providing consultation.

8. The nurse specialist critically evaluates new knowledge related to health and developmental services.

Standard IV. Collegiality

The nurse working in the field of DD and/or MR contributes to the professional development of peers, colleagues, and others.

Measurement Criteria

1. The nurse assists others in identifying their educational needs and communicates information to them.

2. The nurse provides professional peers, unlicensed assistive personnel, and families with constructive feedback regarding the care they provide.

3. The nurse develops and presents educational material to others in the area of health and wellness as it pertains to individuals with DD and/or MR and their families. This may be in the form of consultation to other disciplines or organizations or through speaking and writing for professional refereed journals and/or books.

Standard V. Ethics

The nurse's decisions and actions on behalf of individuals with DD and/or MR are determined in an ethical manner.

Measurement Criteria

1. The nurse's practice is guided by the *Code for Nurses with Interpretive Statements* (ANA, 1985) and other relevant standards.

2. The nurse respects the person's right to self-determination and includes the person in decisions as appropriate to his or her capacity to reason and the degree of impact of the decision on the person's life. Family or other legally designated guardians are included in decision-making, or make the decision as surrogate decision-makers when appropriate.

3. The nurse acts as an advocate for individuals with DD and/or MR and their families when appropriate.

4. The nurse teaches individuals and families to advocate for themselves.

5. The nurse refers the person to a qualified advocate for persons with DD and/or MR when appropriate.

6. The nurse assures the individual's and family's right to privacy and confidentiality, except when consent to share information has been given by the individual and/or legal guardian.

7. The nurse engages in therapeutic relationships and maintains professional boundaries so that the independence of individuals with DD and/or MR and their families is assured.

8. The nurse delivers care in a nonjudgmental and nondiscriminatory manner that is sensitive to cultural and ethnic diversity among individuals with DD and/or MR and their families.

9. The nurse identifies ethical problems that occur within the practice environment and seeks available resources to formulate ethical decisions.

10. The nurse works to prevent and promptly respond to signs of abuse.

11. The nurse minimizes conflicts of interest between the individual and the surrogate decision-maker when they occur and acts in the best interest of the individual with DD and/or MR.

12. The nurse assists the family in the guardianship process when appropriate.

13. The nurse assists in identifying the most appropriate living arrangements for the person in the least restrictive environment.

14. The nurse contributes to the educational program recommendations and advocates for the least restrictive environment to maximize the person's potential.

15. The nurse contributes to the service program recommendations and advocates for the most appropriate employ-

ment environment. The nurse assists in identifying reasonable accommodations to maximize the person's productivity and satisfaction.

16. The nurse serves as an advocate to ensure that individuals have access to health care that provides continuity and is provided by a practitioner competent to manage the health concerns of persons with DD and/or MR.

17. The nurse participates in the decision-making process to assure that the use of medications; treatment routines; health, developmental, and behavioral assessments; dietary regimens; and/or therapies is appropriate.

18. The nurse facilitates the person's expression of sexuality in a manner that is consistent with the person's native culture, religious upbringing, and level of maturity, and provides counseling as appropriate. The nurse contributes to an environment that protects the person from sexual exploitation in home, school, work, and community.

19. The nurse advocates for appropriate leisure activities acceptable to the person.

20. The nurse advocates for the person's exercise of religious freedom, so that the person can participate (or not participate) in the religious community of his or her choice as appropriate to that person's developmental level.

21. The nurse assists in the referral process for local, state, regional, and federal assistance programs.

Standard VI. Collaboration

The nurse collaborates with the client, family, significant others, and health care providers in planning, implementing, and evaluating individual or community-based services.

Measurement Criteria

1. The nurse administrator participates with other administrative team members in policy-making and in overall agency and community planning, implementation, and evaluation of services to and programs for individuals with DD and/or MR.

2. With other members of the interdisciplinary team, the nurse assists the individual with DD and/or MR in making decisions, when appropriate.

3. The nurse working in the field of DD and/or MR recognizes and respects the contributions of the individual, the family, professional colleagues, and community representatives.

4. The nurse articulates knowledge and skills so that they may be coordinated with the contributions of the individual, family or significant others, and other professional colleagues working with an individual with DD and/or MR or a community-based agency.

5. The nurse collaborates with the individual and family or significant others, and supports the efforts of clients and families in making appropriate decisions about utilization of resources.

6. The nurse makes referrals and provides follow-up care to assure the quality and continuity of care.

7. The nurse collaborates and negotiates with community leaders, public/private agency administrators, professional colleagues, and advocacy or peer support groups to enhance individual or systems capacity for providing quality care.

8. The nurse in the field of DD and/or MR collaborates with other disciplines in teaching, consultation, management, and research activities as opportunities arise.

Standard VII. Research

The nurse contributes to nursing and the field of DD and/or MR through the participation in and use of research.

Measurement Criteria

1. The nurse analyzes research and theory relevant to the practice of nursing in the field of DD and/or MR.

2. The nurse shares current theoretical information and research findings with families, peers, students, other professionals, and advocacy groups.

3. The nurse uses interventions substantiated by scientific research.

4. The nurse participates in research as appropriate to the nurse's position, education, experience, and practice environment. Such activities may include—
    -   identification of clinical problems suitable for nursing research
    -   participation in data collection
    -   participation in unit, organization, or community research committees or programs
    -   sharing research activities with others
    -   conducting research and disseminating findings
    -   critiquing research for application to practice
    -   using research findings in the development of policies, procedures, and guidelines for care of individuals with DD and/or MR
    -   consulting with research experts and colleagues as necessary
    -   program evaluation.

5. The nurse participates in human-subject protection activities as appropriate and is particularly cognizant of the vulnerability and possible exploitation of individuals with DD and/or MR.

Standard VIII. Resource Utilization

The nurse working in the field of DD and/or MR considers and evaluates factors related to safety, effectiveness, and cost in planning and delivering care.

Measurement Criteria

1. The nurse participates in community needs assessments and develops strategies to address individual and family or population-based needs, concerns, and priorities.

2. The nurse participates in developing, implementing, and evaluating needed health care systems or programs that provide services to individuals with DD and/or MR and their families.

3. The nurse discusses benefits and costs of treatment options with the client, family, or significant others, and other providers as appropriate.

4. The nurse assists the client, family, or significant others in identifying and securing appropriate services available to address health care needs.

5. The nurse assigns tasks and delegates care based on the needs of the client or program and the knowledge and skills of the selected provider.

6. The nurse participates in ongoing resource utilization review.

GLOSSARY

"Best Interests" Standard—Surrogate decision-makers may not know a person's wishes under particular circumstances due to never being told or to the fact that the individual was never competent. "In these situations, surrogate decision-makers will be unable to make a valid substituted judgment; instead, they must try to make a choice for the person that seeks to implement what is in that person's best interests by reference to more objective, societally shared criteria. The surrogate must take into account such factors as the relief of suffering, the preservation or restoration of functioning, and the quality as well as the extent of life sustained" (President's Commission for the Study of Ethical Problems in Medicine and Biomedical and Behavioral Research, 1983, pp. 134-135).

Criteria—Measurable objectives related to the specific standard of nursing practice.

Nursing—The diagnosis and treatment of human responses to health and illness (ANA, 1995).

Standard—Standards are authoritative statements by which the nursing profession describes responsibilities for which its practitioners are accountable. These standards reflect the values and priorities of the profession and provide direction for nursing practice and a framework for the evaluation of practice. Standards define the nursing profession's accountability to the public and the client outcomes for which nurses are responsible (ANA, 1991).

Standards of Care—Authoritative statements which encompass the minimal competency level of nursing care and involve the process of assessment, diagnosis, outcome identification, planning, implementation, and evaluation.

Standards of Nursing Practice—Authoritative statements that encompass the art and science of nursing or the quality of care and performance level of nursing practice. The two areas that make up the Standards of Nursing Practice are the Standards of Care and the Standards of Professional Performance.

Standards of Professional Performance—Authoritative statements that encompass the minimal competency level of professional performance and involve the role functions of quality of care, performance appraisal, education, collegiality, ethics, collaboration, research, and resource utilization.

"Substituted Judgment" Standard—"The substituted judgment standard requires the surrogate decision-maker to reach a decision that the incapacitated person would have made if [he or she] were able. This standard can only be used if the person was once capable of developing a view relevant to the particular circumstance" (President's Commission for the Study of Ethical Problems in Medicine and Biomedical and Behavioral Research, 1983, pp. 132-133).

REFERENCES

American Nurses Association. (1995). *Nursing's Social Policy Statement*. Washington, DC: American Nurses Association.

American Nurses Association. (1994a). *Implementation of Nursing Practice Standards and Guidelines*. Kansas City, MO: American Nurses Association.

American Nurses Association. (1994b). *Standards of Psychiatric-Mental Health Clinical Nursing Practice*. Washington, DC: American Nurses Association.

American Nurses Association. (1991). *Standards of Clinical Nursing Practice*. Washington, DC: American Nurses Association.

American Nurses Association. (1986). *Standards of Community Health Nursing Practice*. Kansas City, MO: American Nurses Association.

American Nurses Association. (1985). *Code for Nurses with Interpretive Statements*. Washington, DC: American Nurses Association.

Austin, J., Challela, M., Huber, C., Sciarillo, W., & Stade, C. (1987). *Standards for the Clinical Nurse Specialist in Developmental Disabilities/Handicapping Conditions*. Washington, DC: American Association of University Affiliated Programs.

Brandt, P.A. (1993). "Negotiation and Problem-Solving Strategies: Collaboration between Families and Professionals." *Infants and Young Children*, 5 (4), 78-84.

Brown, M.C., & Roth, S.P. (1994). "Nursing Assessment and Diagnosis." In S.P. Roth & J.S. Morse (Eds.). *A Life-Span Approach to Nursing Care for Individuals with Developmental Disabilities* (pp. 119-146). Baltimore, MD: Paul H. Brookes Publishing.

Consensus Committee and the Maternal-Child Health Bureau. (1994). *Standards of Nursing Practice for the Care of Children and*

Adolescents with Special Health and Developmental Needs.
Washington, DC: Maternal-Child Health Bureau.

Feeg, V.D. (1994). "Foreword." In S.P. Roth & J.S. Morse (Eds.). *A Life-Span Approach to Nursing Care for Individuals with Developmental Disabilities* (pp. x). Baltimore, MD: Paul H. Brookes Publishing.

Huber, D. (1996). *Leadership and Nursing Care Management.* Philadelphia, PA: Saunders.

Luckasson, R., Coulter, D.L., Polloway, E.A., Reiss, S., Schalock, R.L., Snell, M.E., Spitalnik, D.M., & Stark, J.A. (1992). *Mental Retardation: Definition, Classification, and Systems of Supports* (9th ed.). Washington, DC: American Association on Mental Retardation.

Morse, J.S. (1994). "An Overview of Developmental Disabilities Nursing." In S.P. Roth & J.S. Morse (Eds.). *A Life-Span Approach to Nursing Care for Individuals with Developmental Disabilities* (pp. 19-58). Baltimore, MD: Paul H. Brookes Publishing.

Natvig, D. (1996). "A Practice Model for Nursing in Developmental Disabilities." *The South Carolina Nurse*, 2(3), 14-15.

President's Commission for the Study of Ethical Problems in Medicine and Biomedical and Behavioral Research. (1983). *Deciding to Forego Life-Sustaining Treatment.* Washington, DC: U.S. Government Printing Office.

Russell, F.F., & Free, T.A. (1994). "The Nurse's Role in Habilitation." In S.P. Roth & J.S. Morse (Eds.). *A Life-Span Approach to Nursing Care for Individuals with Developmental Disabilities* (pp. 59-88). Baltimore, MD: Paul H. Brookes Publishing.

Society of Pediatric Nurses and American Nurses Association. (1996). *Statement on the Scope and Standards of Pediatric Clinical Nursing Practice.* Washington, DC: American Nurses Association.

Steadham, C.I., & Frank, J. (1993). "Role of Professional Nurses in the Field of Developmental Disabilities." *Mental Retardation*, 31, 179-181.

U.S. House of Representatives. (1978). *Conference Report: Comprehensive Rehabilitation Services Amendments of 1978* (Report No. 95-1780, pp. 51-52). Washington, DC: U.S. Government Printing Office.

Washington State Task Force. (1993). *Children with Special Health Care Needs: Guidelines for Nursing Practice*. (Training Grant Project 909). Seattle, WA: University of Washington, Parent & Child Nursing Department and State of Washington Bureau of Maternal-Child Health and Resources Development, Public Health Service, Department of Health and Human Resources.

ACKNOWLEDGMENTS

The Nursing Division of the American Association on Mental Retardation and the American Nurses Association would like to personally thank those who contributed their valuable time and talents to the *Statement on the Scope and Standards for the Nurse Who Specializes in Developmental Disabilities and/or Mental Retardation:*

Task Force on the Development of the *Statement on the Scope and Standards for the Nurse Who Specializes in Developmental Disabilities and/or Mental Retardation*

Wendy M. Nehring, RN, PhD, FAAMR
Shirley P. Roth, RN, MSN, FAAMR
Deborah Natvig, RN, PhD
Joyce S. Morse, RN, MA, PNP, FAAMR
Teresa Savage, RN, PhD
Marilyn Krajicek, RN, EdD, FAAN

Contributors

Marisa Brown, RN, MSN
Teresa Free, RN, PhD
Athleen Godfrey, RN, MS, FAAN
Bette Keltner, RN, PhD, FAAN
Betty Rice, RN, MSN
Cordelia Robinson, RN, PhD
Linda Ross, RN, MA, CPNP
Patricia Rowell, RN, PhD
Fay Russell, RNC, MN, FAAMR

Library of Congress Cataloging-in-Publication Data

American Nurses Association.
   Statement on the scope and standards for the nurse who special-
izes in developmental disabilities and/or mental retardation /
Nursing Division of the American Association on Mental Retardation
[and] American Nurses Association.
             p.   cm.
   Includes bibliographical references.
   1. Mental retardation—Nursing—Standards. 2. Developmental
disabilities—Nursing—Standards.   I. American Association on
Mental Retardation.   Nursing Division.   II. Title.
   [DNLM: 1. Developmental Disabilities—nursing. 2. Mental
Retardation—nursing. 3. Psychiatric Nursing—methods.
4. Psychiatric Nursing—standards.   WY 160 A5125s 1998]
   RC570.A66 1998
   610.73'68—DC21
   DNLM/DLC
   for Library of Congress   98-17361
                                                       CIP

Published by
American Nurses Publishing
600 Maryland Avenue, SW
Suite 100 West
Washington, DC 20024-2571

INDEX

Note: Entries designated by [1998] indicates an entry from the 1998 *Statement on the Scope and Standards for the Nurse Who Specializes in Developmental Disabilities and/or Mental Retardation*, which is reproduced in Appendix A.

Documentation
    assessment and, 19
    collaboration and, 40, 41
    coordination of care and, 27
    diagnosis and, 21
    education and, 36
    evaluation and, 31, 32
    implementation and, 26
    outcomes identification and, 22
    planning and, 24
    quality of practice and, 33, 35

E

Early intervention, 5, 6, 51
    See also Interventions
Economic issues. *See* Cost control
Education of I/DD nurses
    collegiality and, 38
    curriculum, 9, 11, 12, 14–15, 17
    historical background, 3, 4, 5, 6
    interdisciplinary process and, 11, 12
    leadership and, 49
    research and, 45
    standard of professional performance,
        36, 54
        [1998], 96–97
    See also Professional development
Education of patients and families
    collaboration and, 40, 41
    decision-making and, 9
    health promotion and, 7, 28
    I/DD nursing and, 4, 12, 13, 14, 17
    legislation, 5
    planning and, 25
    See also Family; Health teaching
        and health promotion; Individual-
        ized education plan; Patient
Employment, 14, 43
    plan, 52
    See also Vocational development
Environment
    collegiality and, 38
    coordination of care and, 27
    ethics and, 43
    inclusion and, 52
    leadership and, 49
    least restrictive, 53

    normalization and, 53
    quality of practice and, 34
    resource utilization and, 47
Ethics
    codes, *vii*, 42
    genomics and, 8
    I/DD and, 6–7, 9
    outcomes identification and, 22
    quality of practice and, 33
    research and, 46
    technology and, 8
    standard of professional performance,
        42–44, 54
        [1998], 94–96
Evaluation, 10, 12, 14
    certification and, 13
    collaboration and, 41
    standard of care [1998], 88–89
    standard of practice, 31–32, 53
Evidence-based practice, 17, 18
    assessment and, 19
    consultation and, 29
    education and, 36
    health promotion and, 28
    implementation and, 26
    leadership and, 50
    outcomes identification and, 22
    planning and, 25
    prescriptive authority and, 30
    quality of practice and, 34
    See also Research

F

Family
    assessment and, 5, 19
    collaboration and, 40, 41
    consultation and, 29
    coordination of care and, 27, 51
    diagnosis and, 21
    ethics and, 42, 43
    evaluation and, 31, 32
    I/DD nursing and, *vii*, 3, 4, 5, 13
    Individualized Family Service Plan,
        52
    measurement criteria for, 79–80,
        81–82, 82–83, 84, 86–87, 88
    outcomes identification and, 22, 23

Implementation (*continued*)
 planning and, 24
 quality of practice and, 34
 standard of care [1998], 86–87
 standard of practice, 26–30, 53
Inclusion, 13, 14
 defined, 52
Inclusive care [1998], 67
Individualized Education Plan (IEP), 7, 52
 [1998], 77
Individualized Family Service Plan (IFSP),
 7, 52
 [1998], 77
Individualized Habilitation Plan (1998;
 IHP), 77
Individualized Health Plan (IHP), 7
 [1998], 77
Individualized Plan for Employment
 (IPE), 7, 52
Individualized Transition Plan (ITP), 7,
 52
Information. *See* Data collection
Institutional care, 1, 3
Intellectual and developmental disabilities (I/DD)
 adolescents with, *vii*, 4, 6, 11, 14, 52
 adults with, *vii*, 5, 11, 14, 52
 children with, 3, 4, 6, 8, 10–11, 52
 employment and, 14, 43, 52
 prenatal, 8, 11
 sexuality and, 44
 social biases against, *vii–viii*, 3–4, 7,
 8, 13
 special needs, 1, 9–10, 51
 technology and, 8, 12, 13, 40, 41
 transitional care, 4, 7, 11, 14, 52
 See also I/DD nursing; Advanced
 Practice Registered Nurse in I/DD;
 Professional registered nurse in
 I/DD
Interdisciplinary healthcare, 9, 10, 13
 advanced practice and, 12
 assessment and, 19
 collaboration and, 40, 41, 51
 collegiality and, 38–39
 coordination of care and, 27, 51
 defined, 53

diagnosis and, 21
early intervention and, 51
education and, 4, 11
ethics and, 42, 43
family and, 7
health promotion and, 28
implementation and, 26
leadership and, 49, 50
outcomes identification and, 22, 23
patient and, 7
person-centered care, 53
planning and, 24, 25, 52
quality of practice and, 34
resource utilization and, 47
[1998], 67, 78
See also Collaboration
Internet, 10, 15, 28
Interventions, 12, 14
 developmental screening and, 51
 implementation and, 26
 Individualized Family Service Plan
 and, 52
 patient and, 7
 planning and, 25
 resource utilization and, 47
 See also Early intervention

K
Kennedy, President John F., 3, 4

L
Laws, statutes, and regulations, 17
 advocacy and, 12
 ethics and, 42
 evaluation and, 31
 outcomes identification and, 22
 patient and, 7, 9
 planning and, 24
 prescriptive authority and, 30
 professional practice evaluation
 and, 37
 [1998], 70–71
 See also Ethics
Leadership, 9
 advanced practice and, 12
 coordination of care and, 27
 resource utilization and, 47

Patient (*continued*)
coordination of care and, 27, 51
diagnosis and, 21
ethics and, 42, 43, 44
evaluation and, 31, 32
health promotion and, 28
I/DD nursing and, 13
measurement criteria for, 79–80,
81–82, 82–83, 84, 86–87, 88
outcomes identification and, 22, 23
planning and, 24
prescriptive authority and, 30
professional practice evaluation
and, 37
relationship with I/DD nurse, 42
resource utilization and, 47
[1998], 68, 70–71
See also Family; Phenomena of
concern to I/DD nursing
Performance appraisal (1998 standard),
92–93
Person-centered care, *vii*, 7, 13
defined, 53
outcomes identification and, 22
planning and, 24
Perceptions of disabilities, 7
Phenomena of concern to I/DD nursing,
6–9
listed, 7
[1998], 68–69
See also Family; Patient
Planning, 10, 12
collaboration and, 40, 41
consultation and, 29
diagnosis and, 21
evaluation and, 31, 32
family and, 5
leadership and, 49
outcomes identification and, 22
resource utilization and, 48
standard of care [1998], 84–85
standard of practice, 24–25, 53
Policy. *See* Healthcare policy
Practice settings, 11, 12–13, 17
Preceptors. *See* Mentoring
Prescriptive authority and treatment
standard of practice, 30

Prevention, 14
health promotion and, 28
planning and, 24
Privacy. *See* Confidentiality
Process, nursing, 6
Professional development, 17
collegiality and, 38
education and, 36
leadership and, 49
professional practice evaluation
and, 37
shortage of nurses, 14–15
[1998], 64
See also Education; Leadership
Professional performance. *See* Standards
of professional performance
Professional practice evaluation
collegiality and, 38
education and, 36
health promotion and, 28
standard of professional performance,
37, 54
[1998], 92–93
Professional registered nurse in I/DD
assessment, 19
collaboration, 40–41
collegiality, 38–39
consultation, 29
coordination of care, 27
diagnosis, 21
education, 9, 36
ethics, 42–44
evaluation, 31, 32
health teaching and health promotion, 28
historical background, 6
implementation, 26
leadership, 49, 50
outcomes identification, 22
planning, 24, 25
professional practice evaluation, 37
qualifications, 9–10
quality of practice, 33–35
research, 45, 46
resource utilization, 47–48
scope of practice, 9–10
[1998], 72